THE STORAGE BOOK

THE STORAGE BOOK

Over 250 inspirational ideas for creating stylish home storage

CYNTHIA INIONS

MITCHELL BEAZLEY

First published in Great Britain in 1997. Reprinted 2000.
by Mitchell Beazley, an imprint of Octopus Publishing Group Limited
2-4 Heron Quays
London E14 4JP

Editor **Julia North**
Senior Art Editor **Susan Downing**
Stylist **Cynthia Inions**
Designer **Tony Spalding**
Production **Rachel Lynch**
Illustrator **Claire Davies**

Executive Editor **Judith More**
Executive Art Editor **Janis Utton**

A CIP record for this book is available from the British Library

ISBN 1 85732 725 X

The publishers have made every effort to ensure that all instructions given in this
book are accurate and safe but they cannot accept liability for any resulting injury,
damage or loss to either person or property, whether direct or consequential and
howsoever arising. The author and publishers will be grateful for any information
which will assist them in keeping future editions up to date.

Typset in Gill Sans
Index complied by Hilary Bird
Printed and bound in China

contents

introduction

below Inexpensive clear and opaque plastic products in plain and simple style offer multiple storage solutions in living areas, garages and workshops. (Unit from Muji.)

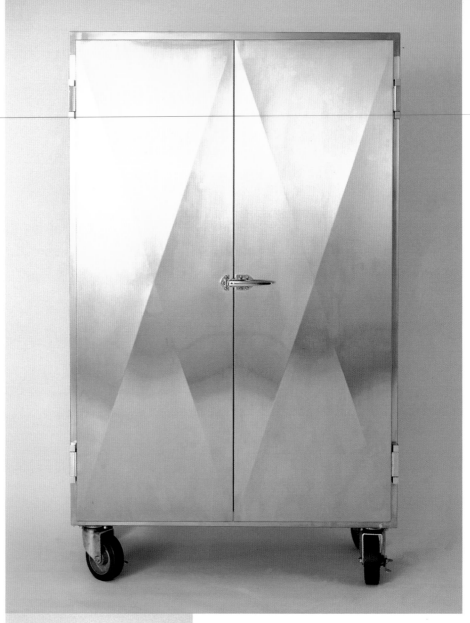

left Use ex-industrial or office fixtures and fittings as storage items. Here, a clothing locker from a public swimming pool is given new status as a key storage item in an open-plan New York apartment.

below Modern manufacturers constantly re-work traditional storage concepts such as roll-top desks or decorative armoires in keeping with multi-functional homes. (Carlo Madera bureau.)

left An inventive alternative to traditional jars for storing herbs and spices, this is a simple combination of polythene bag and an airtight clip. Hang multiple bags in a horizontal line.

above State of the art design and basic practicality can be effectively combined in singular storage items like this impressive Stanley cupboard. (Manufactured by Dialogica.)

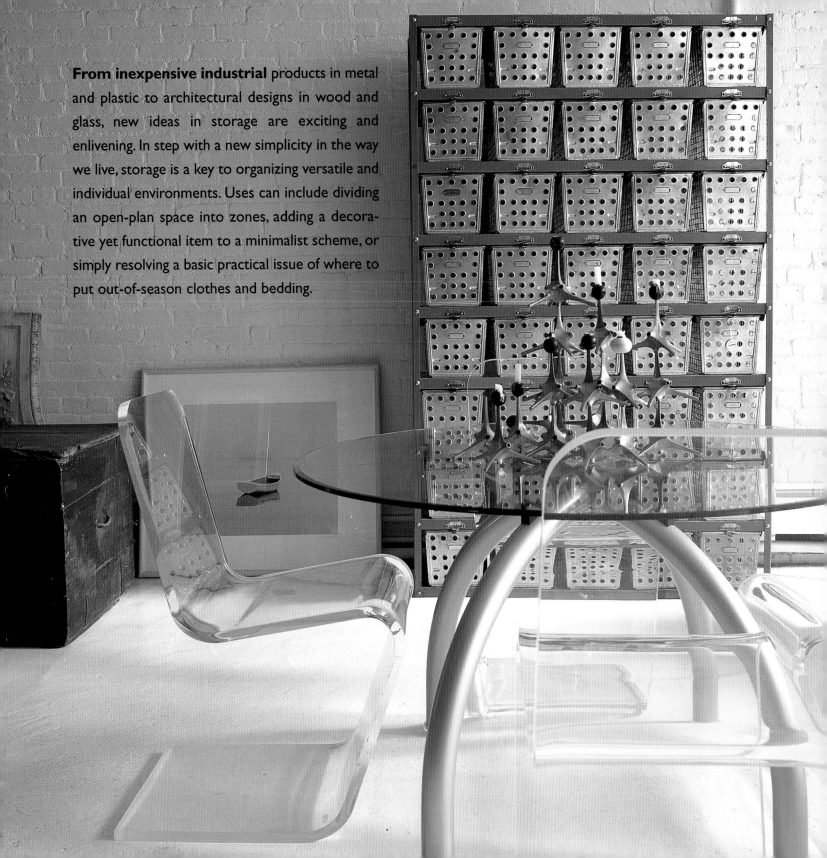

From inexpensive industrial products in metal and plastic to architectural designs in wood and glass, new ideas in storage are exciting and enlivening. In step with a new simplicity in the way we live, storage is a key to organizing versatile and individual environments. Uses can include dividing an open-plan space into zones, adding a decorative yet functional item to a minimalist scheme, or simply resolving a basic practical issue of where to put out-of-season clothes and bedding.

Of the many inspirational and practical storage solutions to revolutionize kitchens, liberate bedrooms and transform living space, some will meet your current requirements exactly while others will need a little modification to fit in perfectly.

Some schemes will suggest a whole new way to live. Perhaps it is time to review and re-organize your domestic environment. Yet before investing in new storage or a structural re-think, begin with a critical edit of everything you possess from kitchen utensils, clothing, books and electrical equipment to furniture and fixtures and fittings.

Simplicity, freedom and a sense of space are not about finding a place to store every single thing. They are about identifying what is essential, functional and inspirational, keeping these elements and giving away, selling or recycling everything else. Consider efficient industrial shelving when planning kitchens; simplify living space with modular storage units for everything from tableware to CD players and books; or screen all your clothes and bedlinen behind translucent sliding glass panels in bedrooms.

Of the many inspirational ideas in this book, the majority can slot with ease into your home to solve difficult storage problems.

above Semi-transparent doors or sliding panels signal an exciting direction in modern storage design, as seen in this impressive cupboard by Maarten Van Severen.

right Dynamic sculptural forms or artistic storage items in wood, glass or stone add a welcome organic element to minimalist environments.

left A preference for combining kitchen and dining areas places a new emphasis on kitchen planning and design. Opt for an efficient easy-to-maintain system with ample hideaway storage to provide a simple but welcoming environment. (Mediterranea by Arc Linea.)

left New designs like this journal rack offer fresh thinking on conventional storage. For alternative ad hoc solutions, use filing cabinets for clothing or metal dustbins for laundry to add vitality to everyday storage solutions.

storage with style

period
style

Grand memorials to a different age, period storage pieces can work within a contemporary interior if you adopt a minimalist approach. Unless you favour living in historically faithful surroundings, cut back or pack away ornaments, simplify decoration with plain colours and install impressive storage items that have a degree of formality and symmetry – ideally a single expansive piece for every situation. For example, a good-size armoire can provide ample storage for books, glassware, foodstuffs, clothing or electronic equipment in just about any setting. A set of drawers is equally versatile, while colonial-style chests and wicker hampers provide extra small-scale storage.

left An antique set of drawers is the main storage item in a former library of a New York conversion. It stands formally at one end of the main room to define a writing and reading space. A packing trunk and ethnic baskets store paperwork. (Design: Tricia Foley.)

above Simple log baskets either side of an imposing stone and carved-wood fire surround fulfil an essential storage function. They also provide inexpensive alternatives to traditional ornamental containers. (Design: Tricia Foley.)

left Too precious and formal to use for food, a period silver platter makes an imaginative cutlery store. Decorative and practical, it can be transferred easily from kitchen shelf to any table setting.

Simplicity and freedom from clutter was the defining feature of a Shaker dwelling. Shaker homes were havens of orderliness, in tune with strict spiritual beliefs. For believers, living as large communal families and sharing everything, it was essential that even the smallest household item had a place where everyone would know where to find it, use it and put it back ready for the next person. Mother Ann, founder of the Shakers in North America in the 1770s, set out directives for this orderly way of life. Her guidelines were plain common sense: "Provide places for all your things so that you may know where to find them at any time, day or night."

shaker style

left Peg rails can take on a different use in every room. Thread loops of string or leather rope through shelf units and hook them over peg rails in kitchens, bathrooms and halls for small-scale storage.

below These sculptural storage boxes and bowls are as appropriate to a period dwelling as a modern interior. Colour-code individual items to identify what is inside.

above Saucepans and shelves for spice jars hang from a peg rail, making them easily accessible for cooking and food preparation. Built-in kitchen cupboards provide a place for everything in a simple arrangement of multi-sized drawers under an oiled-wood worktop.

left A peg rail running around a plain wall is a key feature of a Shaker-style interior for storing essential everyday items. Shakers did not believe in display for the sake of it, so if you do not use it often, do not hang it on a peg rail.

The simplicity and the honest functionalism of historic Shaker dwellings, with a delight in space and respect for nature's gifts, is essential inspiration for contemporary interiors. Simple storage along Shaker lines organizes objects according to common sense: each item is given a place appropriate to how often it is used, or relevant to its size and weight. Storage furniture can include floor-to-ceiling cupboards and chests of drawers in pine, maple and cherrywood for storing all kinds of household items from tableware to clothing. Peg rails around every room provide easy-access hanging space for brooms and everyday items, keeping the floor clear and easy to sweep. Freestanding furniture is best kept to a minimum, with only as many chairs as people to sit on them. When chairs are not in use, store them off the floor on peg rails. Everything should play a part efficiently and harmoniously – another key Shaker directive that is as relevant now as it was to Mother Ann in the 1770s.

left Shaker ladderback chairs are designed for hanging out of the way on hooks when not in use. Make sure that your peg rail is securely fixed to a wall before you hang any kind of chair in this way.

country
style

above Hanging by a nail on a brick wall in a utility room, a shallow basket is a useful container for a jumble of pegs and sticks. It exemplifies the practicality of country style.

right A country kitchen cutlery tray with central division neatly frames and separates antique knives and forks for decorative and functional storage.

above Redundant food safes with fine wire mesh fixed onto wooden frames make useful storage cupboards for china, tablelinen and dry food or cans.

right A wooden bucket with individual staves bound in place by a metal hoop is a convenient store for kitchen utensils and makes a decorative feature of everything it contains.

From pocket-sized cottages to grand country houses, or even urban interiors with an identity crisis, the traditions at the heart of country style – mixing, not matching – will apply. This means the freedom to combine inexpensive junk-shop finds, homespun antiques, special pieces that have a family history and anything you like the look of.

left In this informal New York apartment, decoration is in homespun-style. A ceramic dish overflowing with family photographs and a painted box that serves as a letter-store provide personal effects with originality and spirit.

below A French wire basket split into sections provides simple but effective storage for glasses. Stack this type of lightweight container with glasses, bottles of olive oil and jars of chutney or spices and carry directly to the table – indoors or out.

right Strong lines on simple furniture are key to the appeal of country-style interiors. This kitchen dresser provides ample storage for all kitchen items, plus additional space to display a collection of antique china.

Adhering to a single period style – or even choosing furniture from one country of origin – will not result in a typically informal country-style mix. To get the look right, start with distinctive basics – for kitchens, perhaps an Italian scrubbed table with a cutlery drawer and an English dresser. As a less conventional alternative, mix an individual shelf unit with a contrasting set of drawers. For sitting rooms, look out for North European painted food safes; these are ideal for books and hi-fi equipment. Decorative Spanish or French armoires provide flexible storage in country-style interiors. Visit markets and auctions and consider the hidden potential of stripping or painting anything you see. Keep a set of room measurements with you before you buy.

Once you have decided on your main pieces of country-style storage furniture and installed them in your interior, you can add the smaller items: traditional ceramics, decorative metalware and anything craft-orientated, like hand-made boxes. For inexpensive solutions, check out local markets or shops for vegetable boxes or wooden crates – as these are perfect for small-scale kitchen storage.

In a radical break with traditions in craft and ornamentation, modernist designs from 1910 to the 1950s were influenced by new technology. The bold architectural shapes of modernist pieces – mass produced from industrial plastics, plywood and steel – still generate a buzz and exert a powerful influence on contemporary designs. Many originals continue in production so it is possible to buy the real thing. Alternatively, collect classics from dealers or markets, track down inexpensive high street equivalents or take inspiration from the colours and simple shapes of these pieces to revamp existing storage items with metal doors, new handles and paint.

contemporary
inspiration

below Highly architectural and colourful, Charles Eames' storage cabinet combines function and form. In a living area, such a piece can provide useful storage for electrical equipment and books.

right In this New York galley kitchen, built-in storage units and appliances are ranged along one wall. This creates a space for table and chairs. (Architects: Fernlund & Logan.)

left Inspired by mass-produced designs from the 1950s, this aluminium wall track system with organic-looking brackets provides an architectural support for heavy glass shelving. (Design: Ali Tayar, Parallel Design.)

below The Isoken donkey provides compact multi-storage for living room paraphernalia, including magazines, newspapers and books, in lightweight sculptural plywood.

right Post-war Scandinavian design brings a modernist perspective to a New York apartment. A teak cupboard stores CDs in an open-plan area. (Architects: Solveig Fernlund & Neil Logan.)

left To modernists, metal in design is the equivalent of concrete in architecture – bold and essential. This revamp to replace wood veneer cupboard doors with inexpensive metal gives an ordinary kitchen-in-a-corridor a dynamic new look.

left The graphic box-like dimensions of a 1950s Knoll teak cabinet with painted steel legs is offset by traditional panelling. The glass vases are modern. For modernist storage on a budget, fix square kitchen wall cupboards to the wall at sideboard height. If necessary, customize them further with paint or a change of handles.

Storage units in the spirit of modernism have a utilitarian simplicity. Many contemporary geometric or modular designs encompass this industrial style, from box-like television cabinets to cubic bookcases. Put together a wall of cubes with interchangeable solid and glass doors and create your own modernist version. Leave some units open, with or without shelves. A strong geometric frame will overpower any disorder within, so a typical jumble of books and magazines will not look out of place.

Explore the potential of box-like wall cupboards. Kitchen suppliers usually offer a good selection. Install a row along a hallway, bedroom or living room at sideboard height with invisible fixings. Place one cupboard in a bathroom for toiletries, or make a square of four in a living room to store books or videos – perhaps paint each cupboard a different colour, or experiment with one colour for the frame and different colours for each door.

Even if your budget does not run to new designs, it is possible to enjoy the poetic plainness of the modern movement. Paint existing cupboards and change handles to simple metal discs, or replace doors with metal or plastic panels.

Beyond presenting almost limitless storage possibilities, ethnic furniture and folk artefacts from around the world seem to exert a magical spell on the post-industrial dwellers of the western world. The bright colours of African baskets or the graphic simplicity of a Japanese chest can add a powerfully primitive or exotic presence to a modern interior. The key to incorporating these elements successfully into new settings is to put them to use as everyday functional storage items.

ethnic
ideas

left A simple 19th-century temple cupboard in teak from West Rajasthan forms part of a collection in David Wainwright's London townhouse. Set on wooden wheels, it transfers easily to a modern interior.

left In the spirit of a cave dwelling, this hewn stone and wood bedside cupboard exerts a powerful force within a Californian interior. Along with kitchen cupboards made out of driftwood-effect planks, wicker baskets and large pots, storage is primitive style.

above Often lacking in modern interiors, decoration is an essential feature of ethnic art. An elaborate artefact or piece of furniture, like this finely carved Nuristani chest offset by a plain backdrop can be both practical and decorative.

right Textile designer Jack Lenor Larsen brings Japanese aesthetics to a collection of ceramics, sculpture and paintings in a New York apartment. Set out with precision on glass shelves within a wooden framework, the collection is seen or hidden thanks to traditional sliding screens.

Inspirational as well as exotic, many ethnic storage ideas originate from ancient cultures and lifestyles and were generally designed to be portable – stacking and nesting baskets from space-conscious Japan; wooden merchants' chests from spice-trading India and woven sacks for clothing and cooking pots from nomadic shepherds from the Atlas mountains.

Still in production, using methods and materials little changed for centuries and easily transportable for travellers and tourists, many bold but simple items transfer well to modern interiors as practical storage solutions.

With furniture – especially wooden items, such as a Mexican sideboard or Korean trunk – it is a good idea to buy imports from specialist dealers close to home. This way, there is less risk of an infestation of exotic insects and, unless the item was shipped very recently, less chance of any climatic shock reactions such as splitting or cracking.

left A majestic antique Japanese *mizuya* in cypress wood, once a silent witness to formal tea ceremonies, provides flexible storage with an array of drawers and sliding panels.

right Hand-woven baskets on open wooden shelves provide decorative and accessible small-scale storage in a New York bedroom. Like a visual index, the pattern, colour and shape of each basket identifies its contents.

above A wall of cupboards are the main feature of this interior. (Courtesy of the Atlanta Historical Society, Inc.)

left Malcolm Temple's ornamental sea chest is made using basic building materials. The frame is carved, stained and varnished MDF and gives an appearance of oriental wood.

Specialist dealers can provide essential back-up and advice about cleaning, repair and restoration. For inexpensive small-scale storage solutions – such as baskets, metalware, wooden bowls and boxes – look in local high street shops, craft stores and craft fairs.

Selecting ethnic storage pieces that are functional as well as decorative is very important. Presenting a Rajasthani temple cupboard as an artistic souvenir will alienate it from its new surroundings, but if you put it into useful service as a linen cupboard or china chest this will make sense of its relocation.

Folk art pieces such as Pueblo Indian water jars or punch-pattern tin boxes from New Mexico can all find new identities as decorative yet essentially practical storage items. Aim to be selective, and think about how ethnic colours and organic shapes will fit in with modern-day industrial precision and exactness. For example, a vast hand-made terracotta grain jar, bargained for with passion in a Moroccan souk, will look quite different on a concrete floor of an urban kitchen. Yet juxtapositions like this can express the power of ethnic design.

hall and porch

hall and
porch

Entrance halls are active transition areas from outside to inside and require effective storage for dropping off or picking up outdoor clothing, a change of footwear, keys, post and perhaps a bicycle. Yet entrance halls should also be welcoming spaces – the first space that you and your visitors will see. So it is important to create a practical, friendly space that is free from clutter or an impassable collection of disorderly clothes or equipment. Ideally, keep the area directly inside the front door clear for quick and easy access and plan any storage solutions to begin beyond the doormat.

left The area behind this sweeping stairway provides storage for cleaning equipment, tools and out-of-season household items. (Architects: Munkenbeck + Marshall.)

above A photographer's trunk converted to domestic storage is in keeping with this industrial-style interior. A collection of antique clocks cleverly inhibits a build-up of clutter.

right An open-plan studio becomes a work/living space with the addition of a bed platform, basic stair and a plexiglass partition to create an office. A hatstand defines the entrance area.

For clothing, umbrellas and bags, there is a huge choice of hooks – from minimalist metal buttons to wooden pegs or very ornate ironwork – that will fit in with contemporary or traditional environments. A wooden or metal pole spanning an alcove can provide useful hanging space if equipped with a good supply of coathangers. If space is available and storage requirements exceed a few coat hooks, line hall walls with cupboards or a mixture of shelves and hanging rails. Concertina doors, sliding panels and roller blinds provide space-conscious alternatives to conventional doors.

Within an open-plan environment consider constructing a simple enclosure to create storage and a sense of division from inner and outer space. A permanent wall or panel, or a less dense sandblasted glass partition to let light pass through, will provide an essential cut-off from the front door and offer a potential storage area with hooks fixed to the wall or a freestanding coatstand or clothes rail.

left A simple sandblasted glass screen conceals a basic clothes rail and contrasts to great effect with a traditional hall table and collection of artefacts. (Architects: Stickland Coombe.)

Hall landings can present welcome and surprising storage possibilities. A bookshelf next to a chair and good light can offer a peaceful reading spot. Alternatively a desk, table or flip-down worktop with shelves for paperwork and files above can provide office or study space. All kinds of cupboards, from armoires to custom-built designs which make the best use of any odd corners, are ideal for overspill or out-of-season clothing, linen, books or sports equipment.

Understair cupboards provide useful storage for bulky items like vacuum cleaners, ironing boards and the usual closet overspill. If there is space, fit a cupboard or shelf for valuable extra storage. If space is really limited, consider the potential for storage above doorways. A plain shelf across the width of a door frame on bracket supports is useful for books. If you want to conceal a jumble of odds and ends, store them in boxes or baskets on the shelf. Consider extending the shelf to run around a landing or along a row of doorways. (It is important to check that this will not create an obstruction before you go ahead.) Alternatively, frame a doorway with narrow shelves from floor to ceiling and create a mini-library.

left A traditional wooden peg rail for coats, and bare floorboards for heavy-duty footwear and walking sticks, adorn this mudroom in Stephen Mack's house. Functional and down-to-earth, the storage here is basic but effective.

above Narrow tables provide ideal storage for busy hallways, and simple structures, like this folding plant table, take up less space than more formal pieces.

left It is hard to beat a peg rail in a hall for practical storage. Perhaps fix two peg rails at different heights for adult and children's outdoor clothing.

open and shut
cases

Whether you spend time reading, listening to music, watching television or flopping on a sofa with friends, flexible storage solutions are the key to organizing a multi-functional and informal living space. From building-block modular units with a mixture of open and shut storage to architectural holes in the wall, modern ideas for accommodating diverse recreational interests will contribute to creating an environment that is both practical and personal.

above This pearwood table with glass top includes a drawer underneath for stacks of magazines and books, and space for games and specialist items or collections. (Arc Linea.)

above This flexible arrangement of storage building blocks features shelves and divisions. Begin with one square and add on new units to meet requirements. (Arc Linea.)

left A simple wooden "D" shelf with steel brackets can look striking. Use it to display selected artbooks, sculptures and personal memorabilia. (Design: Annabelle Selldorf.)

right Simplicity, light and space are key elements in this New York apartment. A simple early 20th-century French cabinet contrasts with a plain shelf for displaying prints. (Design: Vicente Wolf.)

Storing every possession on view can look chaotic and overpower a living space, yet if everything is hidden away a room can appear unwelcoming. For a sense of order with a human touch, mix open and shut storage for entertainment equipment as well as displays of selected personal items.

Individual preference is a good guide when planning what to reveal and what to conceal – especially if you have one main leisure activity. Aim for versatility and variety. For multi-functional spaces, display something of all key interests in open storage and conceal bulky back-up equipment or specialist collections. Alternatively, select specific storage items, perhaps a cabinet or shelf system, for individual activities and divide a living space into recreational zones.

Store collections of CDs, videos or books in a drawer unit, cabinet or a storage system with sliding front panels. Keep a selection of current favourites to hand in either an open rack, single shelf or simple informal stack.

right This spacious living area contains a mixture of open and shut storage. CDs and videos reside in a drawer unit, while African artefacts are displayed on an oak table. (Furniture designer/maker: Andrew Mortada.)

Using open storage to display artefacts, collections, photographs or anything of personal interest that is visually stimulating enlivens any space. Choose a storage system that is relevant to the items that you intend to display. For example, a bold system of parallel wooden shelves is perfect for displaying modern sculpture or black and white photographic prints in a contemporary environment, yet it can overpower a collection of colourful American folk art or Japanese ceramics.

Before opting for a storage system – open shelving or shelves within a framework, perhaps in glass, metal or wood – check weight and space requirements. If a collection of artefacts or electronic equipment is complete, opt for permanent shelving with wall brackets or metal supports; or, for invisible fixings, embed metal rods into the wall and then into the back of wooden shelves.

Lay out everything for display on the floor and map out an arrangement or make a storage plan. Double-check measurements with special attention to depth. Always leave adequate space front and back, especially for equipment with wires and connections.

left An effective contrast of modernity and antiquity in a New York apartment. A display shelf for photographs is an ideal, flexible storage solution. (Design: Vicente Wolf.)

below In keeping with a graphic modern environment, a wall shelf with invisible fixings for artefacts and art presents a clean-cut profile. (Furniture from Arc Linea.)

right A collection of cheap and cheerful figures from South America are given equal prominence on this network of glass shelves within a simple wooden framework.

left A strikingly simple wall-mounted shelving system with tracks and adjustable brackets in anodized aluminium is as visually appealing as the ceramics on display. (Ellen's Brackets by Ali Tayar for Parallel Design.)

Some storage options are in fact architectural solutions – structural add-ons or details which appear to be part of the framework of a space. Ambitious ideas, such as replacing partition walls with floor-to-ceiling storage systems accessible from both sides, or adding a parallel wall next to an existing wall to create storage space in between, require forward planning and imagination. For ideas on this scale, consult an architect for creative input and incorporate any suggestions or recommendations at the initial planning or refurbishment stage for maximum economy and minimal disruption.

For minimalists, the appeal of structural storage is to devise a practical framework for living, free from the clutter of individual items of furniture yet without prohibiting possessions. However, be aware – this level of simplicity will throw into relief anything on display. Keep visible elements either honest and functional or sculptural and artistic; perhaps a compact music system, African figure or Japanese light.

right A desk and video shelf, suspended between a sculptural plaster wall and original metal support, links traditional and modern architectural details in a workshop conversion. (Furniture designer/maker: Andrew Mortada.)

right Basic units are transformed with gold leaf and varnish. Each unit consists of a stack of two individual cupboards, with TV, video and music equipment under lock and key, and children's toys below. (Design: Justin Meath Baker.)

below A sculptural music cupboard in beaten lead, aluminium and wood provides storage for a bank of equipment, and adds a powerful presence in a modern environment. (Weymouth cupboard and CD cabinet by Malcolm Temple.)

Even in high-tech warehouse conversions, on-view entertainment equipment can look too raw and industrial. In a conventional house or apartment, managing this juxtaposition is a challenge. Yet entertainment equipment is now a key element in many living spaces, so aim to incorporate equipment in an accessible yet stylish way.

Function and decoration can be combined in attractive storage items for concealing bulky or incongruous pieces of equipment. Alternatively, customize an existing cupboard. Inexpensive MDF or pine cupboards can be transformed with silver or gold leaf and varnish or architectural moulding. Use contrasting paint colours or cover the item in hessian or thin sheets of zinc or copper; change existing handles to cut-glass spheres or something organic like twigs or found driftwood. For modern eclectics, eccentric gothic-style hand-me-downs, antiquities or anything ethnic will work well, especially in contrast to a modern backdrop. Likewise, contemporary pieces in an historic setting will look singular and impressive. Always give decorative storage items visual prominence and space.

above An oriental-style drawer unit in MDF and resin with solid cast resin legs provides distinctive storage for everyday paperwork, videos and CDs – in bold contrast to a sandblasted brick interior. (Furniture designer/maker: Andrew Mortada.)

left Ideal for concealing entertainment equipment, a traditional New England cabinet provides essential storage in historic style. In addition, a traditional blanket box doubles as table and storage for books and magazines.

right A mini fork-lift device is in keeping with the size statement of TV, video and music system in this apartment. A basket for CDs and videos, with black and white prints on top, offsets this raw industrial style.

below Compact and mobile, a simple storage system with TV platform, video shelf and box for tapes, can be wheeled into position for viewing when needed. (Biblica from Arc Linea.)

If you enjoy watching TV and videos frequently, invest in a sizeable screen and position it for direct viewing. However, a television that sits directly in front of a sofa or in the centre of a general living space can conflict with alternative activities and encourage passive, automatic viewing.

Storing entertainment equipment on trolleys, mobile cabinets or pivoting wall brackets and moving it into position when you want to use it gives you immediate access with the flexibility to do something else without effort. Choose a style of storage to fit in with existing decoration or architecture – perhaps a lightweight aluminium trolley with adjustable shelves, or a low wooden unit with a stacking device for TV and video and a drawer for video tapes. If you tend to favour stark contrasts between high technology and domesticity, opt for heavy-duty fixtures designed for professional studios.

left Compact music systems on lightweight trolleys are ideal to whizz around single-level apartments. (From Habitat.)

right This basket is ideal for transporting your CDs. Keep current favourites on view next to a hi-fi for easy access, and store the bulk of a collection elsewhere. (From The Source.)

Books are an integral personal feature in any living environment – be they in an informal pile on a chair, on individual shelves arranged in graphic colour-coded blocks or as a random selection in an open storage system alongside artefacts and entertainment equipment. Use adjustable shelving units, individual storage cabinets or modular units to accommodate anything from standard paperbacks to out-size art and reference books. With extensive collections, avoid the academic look of book "wallpaper" in a general living area. Instead, partially conceal books behind sliding panels or open and shut storage.

books

above Modular units with open and shut storage can conceal a mass of books and bulky entertainment equipment, while revealing a decorative selection of books and artefacts.

left A bold wooden shelf across an odd space makes a useful and unobtrusive bookshelf. Beware of utilizing every spare bit of space for book storage and thus overpowering a general living area.

above A conventional yet practical storage solution: building a bookcase in an architectural alcove. Use vertical tracks with adjustable shelving for maximum flexibility.

right A country-style wall rack makes convenient storage for magazines, newspapers and paperbacks. As alternative storage for a selection of books, use a basket or compact trolley.

If you can designate space in general living areas for book storage and reading, celebrate with a distinctive storage item – perhaps a rotating book stand or a mobile stainless steel cabinet with internal shelving; or construct a stack or spiral of inexpensive wooden boxes. Simply stand one on top of the other and let the weight of the books act as anchor, or use screws to fix together top and bottom.

Open shelving or low units and cupboards can double up as convenient book storage and partitions within open-plan areas. Alternatively, to keep space free and flexible (especially in conventional set-ups), utilize outer-perimeter storage potential – floor-to-ceiling shelving systems in alcoves or comprehensive wall systems, for example. For a mass of books, store the collection in a shelving system with sliding front panels or doors in wood, metal or semi-transparent glass and reveal different sections at a time. For a similar partial-reveal effect, stretch blank canvas over a light frame and prop up against conventional book shelves.

left In an open-plan apartment, welcoming chairs and a rotating bookstand define a light and spacious reading area.

below Low cupboards or mobile units such as this provide convenient book storage and act as space dividers to create a quiet area for reading.

right A vast Indian bowl is an imaginative storage solution for reference books and magazines, and sits perfectly between home office and general living area.

For a mixture of books and artefacts in open storage, vertical tracks with adjustable shelves or modular building-block systems with various shelving options provide flexible no-fuss solutions.

Tracking systems offer maximum flexibility, especially for big art or reference books. Alternatively, install adjustable shelving within a DIY framework. Fix tracks to the back of the unit or side verticals. Use wood for the frame and either wood, metal or glass for shelving. Depending on the size of the unit and load-bearing capacity of the shelving, insert a vertical panel or track approximately every 50cm/20in. Paint the unit, including the back wall, the same colour as the rest of the room to throw books and artefacts into relief. Or, decorate to emphasize the frame, not the shelf positions within. Perhaps use contrasting paint colours for frame and shelving or fix architraving or facing to the frame.

left Books and artefacts on open shelving provide a decorative display. Paint units the same colour as the surrounding walls to offset ceramics and pieces of art.

right This contemporary version of a cinderblock and plank shelf unit is collapsible and extendable horizontally and vertically with aluminium connector brackets. Design: Ali Tayar.

bedroom

left A wall of built-in cupboards – with wallcovering and panelling to match the rest of the room – provides extensive, invisible bedroom storage.

the closet

left An ornate metal frame with drapes makes a decorative free-standing storage unit. As an alternative to metal, put together a simple wooden frame or box and fix plain canvas banners all around.

above This expandable flexible storage system – with basic steel frame, shelf unit and clothes rail fronted by curtain pole and cotton drapes – provides ample hanging and shelf space.

right A substantial storage solution that makes use of built-in cupboards on either side of a window. Natural blinds, instead of traditional doors, hide clothes and shoes.

Creating the right environment for sleep and relaxation is very important – so plan bedroom storage with special care and attention to detail. If space is at a premium and a bedroom is also an office, gym or alternative television room, then organization and flexible storage are especially critical. A mixture of hanging and drawer or shelf space will provide all the basic storage requirements for clothing. Take into account the ratio of how much hanging to how much shelf space is needed, together with space available and structure or architecture of the environment, to find a workable storage solution.

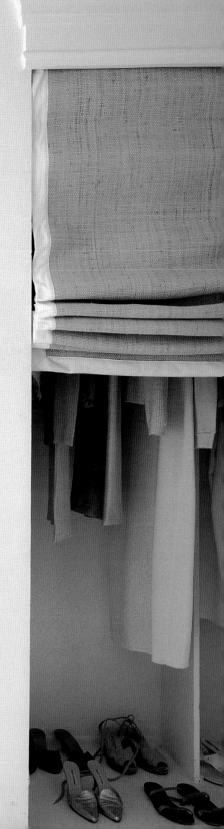

A one-block storage network of inexpensive self-assembly metal, MDF or pine drawers with basic hanging rails and adjustable shelving systems can provide complete bedroom storage. Range the network along one wall or divide in two between two alcoves. Contain everything within an overall framework and conceal with sliding panels, doors or an inexpensive canvas curtain on a metal pole.

Conceal individual storage sections in different ways – for example, hang a linen blind in front of shelves, leave a section of baskets or storage boxes on view and install a sliding mirror panel in front of clothes rails. In period-style interiors where the walls are decorated with panelling or wallpaper, match the cupboard fronts to the rest of the scheme, continue any architraving or skirting and create an invisible wall of storage.

Open storage for clothing is another option – ideal for minimalists or anyone who favours a strict colour code. Avoid overloading open rails with items, or clashing colours and patterns; the effect can be chaotic. Clothing bags, canvas or plastic bags with front zippers, will help to reduce the jumbled effect and protect clothes from dust.

above A metal frame unit with deep drawers provides ample storage for underwear, jumpers, shirts and jeans. Each drawer can be lined with tissue paper to help keep clothes pristine.

below Storing out-of-season jumpers and shirts in a transparent envelope will protect each item from dust in a drawer or open shelf. Bags with canvas backing help clothes "breathe".

above As an original alternative to clothing rails running parallel to a wall, these face-on perspex rails provide compact storage.

right Functional and stylish open storage with perspex rails and sculptural shelf, inspired by Gabriella Ligenza's London hat shop fittings. Plastic boxes store scarves and special items on the top shelf. (Design: Janie Jackson.)

Choose high-quality fittings and fixtures such as sculptural shelves, perspex clothes rails or metal structures if you want open storage in the bedroom. And supplement minimalist hanging rails with additional storage for everyday jumpers, shirts and underwear; a simple line of open baskets, an independent drawer unit or easily accessible shelves will work well. Cardboard or perspex boxes with lids, impractical for everyday use, are ideal for storing less frequently worn or out-of-season clothes.

Explore the possibility of fitting compact drawer units, or a shelf system to store boxes or baskets, within existing closets. Characterful period pieces such as armoires, with only a single rail or perhaps three or four shelves, will benefit from a refit to provide ample storage. Incorporate space-saving devices like a spinning tie-rack on a hook or fix organizers or bags inside doors.

For any additional bedroom storage, offset period pieces with contemporary items such as a perspex trolley with drawers. Be creative when mixing styles and sizes and consider painting or silver-leafing dark wood pieces to lighten any grandiose effect.

left A compact tie spinner neatly stores ties. Utilize small-scale storage solutions like this to improve organization and protect clothing within traditional or contemporary closets.

right An architectural metal structure at one end of this bedroom provides ample hanging space for suit bags with cheap and cheerful brown paper bags below for underwear, jumpers and t-shirts. Design: Justin Meath Baker.

below Moroccan-style drapes and a kilim transform a simple alcove cupboard into a striking feature. If possible, install a wall or ceiling light when partitioning a walk-in storage space.

left Voluminous drawstring sacks with contrasting interlinings make jolly storage for toys. They are easy to transport from one play area to another and ideal for a quick toy sweep when play is over.

right and below An inventive twist on underbed storage: a bed which pulls out from and stores away underneath a magnificent glass display platform revealing a collection of sea treasures. There is ample storage for clothing in lockers and hanging rails either side. This is a compact and inventive design solution which removes the bed as a dominant feature within the room without major disruption or effort. (Architectural design: Charles Rutherfoord.)

bed and
bedside

The style, size and position of a bed is a key factor in organizing space and planning storage solutions in a sleeping environment. Flexible bedroom furniture, such as roll-up futons, beds in cupboards which hinge or pivot out of the way, sofa-beds or bed platforms, can provide valuable extra storage space. But there are many other simple storage ideas, often centred under or beside the bed, that suit conventional arrangements and maximize the sense of space.

right Decorative chairs provide simple storage for everyday clothing and clean laundry. With ample storage elsewhere, witty details like this enliven an interior.

above An American chicken crate makes an inexpensive country-style table and storage box. Do not restore simple crates and boxes, as you run the risk of taking away essential texture and character – simply remove dangerous nails or splinters, and paint or stain.

right An ex-shop display cabinet fits conveniently beneath a window to provide expansive storage space in this bedroom. The contents can be partly concealed by stapling muslin or linen over glass panels or replace clear glass with sand-blasted glass.

Many contemporary bed designs integrate storage space for essential bedside items. Space for books and reading lights can be found within headboards, swivel side tables or vast mattress platforms with run-around, bench-like shelves. For a simple headboard and shelf combination, set a plain divan or bed-base away from the wall, run two long shelves behind, extending on either side of the bed-base, then slot a hardboard panel between the bed-base and shelves. Fix one shelf level with the bed-base and one just below the top of the panel. Paint everything one colour and slide the bed-base up against the panel. Use the top shelf for storing books or to prop up a favourite painting.

As an alternative to traditional pieces such as pot cupboards or blanket boxes, use wicker hampers or travel chests to store spare pillows and out-of-season duvets. Look out for quirky ex-shop display cabinets and line any glass panels with muslin. A colourful hat box is a useful store for photographs, letters or even hats!

left An architectural recess shelf above this bed provides a useful store for essentials, in addition to swivel side tables. Clothing is hidden in a mobile closet with graphic aluminium doors. (Furniture from Ligne Roset.)

Utilizing space under a bed for practical storage is worth every effort. Even if space-saving is a not an issue, it is worth exploiting the potential to store substantial amounts of clothing, bedding or equipment out of sight.

Built-in drawers in bed frames can also provide sensible underbed storage – ideal for shirts, jumpers, spare bedlinen and blankets. If space is tight and side drawers are inconvenient, fit drawers at the foot of the bed for easier access.

As an alternative to built-in storage, combine any high-level bed with independent low-level storage. An MDF or wooden platform (or even a single drawer from a pine chest) on heavy-duty castors provides a good base for storage. Items can either be stored directly on the platform itself, or within storage boxes or baskets placed on top of the platform.

Use boxes with lids to protect clothes from dust and store jumpers and shirts in transparent clothes bags in open baskets or containers; use muslin drawstring liners and seal individual piles, or simply place a linen napkin or tea towel on top. For stability, fix the containers to the platform or platforms with screws or glue.

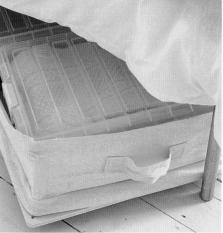

above A custom-built bed with large under-bed drawers for shirts, T-shirts, jumpers and spare bedlinen makes the most of otherwise "dead" space. Two distinctive bedside cabinets, one a practical cubic design and one artistic and decorative, complete this idiosyncratic scheme. (Design: Justin Meath Baker.)

right A DIY bed on a scaffolding frame sits high enough for easy under-bed access. Canvas containers on wheels provide useful additional storage for clothing and blankets.

left Open canvas or cardboard boxes are ideal for underbed storage. To protect clothing from dust, use transparent plastic bags or containers.

bathroom

Include storage ideas at the planning stage of any new bath or shower room. A simple recess shelf in the wall of the shower area for gels and lotions is integral to the design and space in a way that a soap-on-a-rope hanging on a shower is not. If you plan to conceal pipework with a false wall, continue the false wall to the ceiling and create a recess shelving system – either leave open or conceal with a sliding mirror panel or mirror doors.

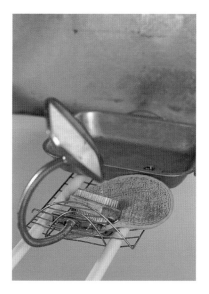

left This bathrack makes clever use of everyday items. A draining rack and roasting tray sit on plastic poles with a flexible rear-view mirror and provide no-fuss storage for a daily shave. (Design: Justin Meath Baker.)

towels and
toiletries

left This metal basket allows a bar of soap to drain and sits at an angle for easy access. As long as soap is not swimming in a puddle of water, any small pot, bowl or basket will work well.

left A perfect compact arrangement for people who get soap in their eyes. Everything is conveniently to hand, from under-basin cupboard to toothbrush rack and linen bag – all in period style.

above Concealing hot and cold water pipes and lavatory cistern behind wood panelling provides a useful run-around shelf for bowls, boxes, mirror and bathroom cupboard.

Standing at a basin to wash requires immediate access to essential items in a compact space – from soap, nailbrush and toothbrush to towels and flannels. The advantage of basins with built-in surrounds – anything from an architectural piece of glass or slab of stone to a traditional wash-stand with a basin set into wood or marble – is all essential items are within easy reach. The disadvantage is that any excessive splashing will soak everything.

To avoid soap or wooden brushes sitting in a puddle of water, store them in a wire basket or use traditional marble dishes with drainage holes in the bottom. To keep toothbrushes dry, stand them in a metal beaker or glass tumbler. For an ad hoc solution, use a sculptural stainless steel colander and store everything together. Specialist bathroom items, like chrome toothbrush holders or soap dishes on wall brackets, are not the only storage options. Transfer a favourite bowl or something basic from the kitchen to provide effective storage with originality.

right A sculptural basin and surround present an imaginative storage solution for soaps and lotions. Glass shelves above the bath provide back-up storage for additional items. (Architects: Munkenbeck + Marshall.)

left In this compact walk-in shower, simple storage items include basic soap dish, mirror cabinet and shelf. Towels and clothing hang on a heated towel rail beside the door. (Architects: Munkenbeck + Marshall.)

right Hanging cylindrical canvas sacks are useful additional storage for the back of a door. Simply thread plastic-coated garden wire through drawstring bags, make a wire loop at one end and hang on simple hooks.

Shelves and cabinets above basins provide practical eye-level storage. Do not limit yourself to bathroom-specific versions. Consider stainless steel racks from kitchen suppliers, wood and metal food safes, or simple open shelf systems, and use as inexpensive alternatives to the standard metal or wood mirrored-door cabinets. Fix a plain mirror above a basin with shelf brackets on either side and use driftwood, slate off-cuts or copper sheeting for inexpensive individual shelving.

If a basin stands in front of a window, utilize the window sill or fix a single shelf below the window frame. Alternatively, stretch high-tension wire across the window frame, using eye plates and a wire tensioner (from sports equipment suppliers), and hook up a mirror and wire basket for toothbrushes, soaps and flannels.

A cupboard under a basin is a very logical use of space. It can conceal pipework and provides ample hideaway storage. Use it to store special items, back-up supplies and cleaning materials.

left Japanese bathing principles in a workshop conversion include cedar bath and separate shower for washing hidden behind a mosaic panel. A simple drawer unit and wall of cupboards store towels and cleaning materials.

Part of the pleasure of getting in a bath is not getting out again until you choose to. Store essentials and lotions within easy reach of the tub. The simplest storage solution is a rack across the bath or a series of metal storage baskets that hang over the side. An inexpensive basket or sand-castle bucket hanging on a tap will work just as well.

If you plan to build a bath surround, aim to incorporate a wide storage shelf — ideally all around the bath or, if space is tight, on one side or one end. If the bath is set against a wall, insert a series of hooks along the wall just above the level of the bath and store supplies in a row of small baskets. A folding chair can provide ideal temporary storage alongside a bath.

Shower enclosures require sensible storage solutions. Plan any storage at the design stage if possible and incorporate an alcove in the wet area for shower gels and shampoo and a dry area for towels and clothing. For example, a shelf above the shower head or, in a compact space, a plastic bin with a lid to keep essentials dry. In simple enclosures, shower racks hanging on a hook or over a temperature control switch will store gels, soaps and brushes within easy reach.

right Incorporate storage ideas at the planning stage of a new bathroom, like this colourful tongue and grooving scheme with built-in bath and shelf surround and recess shelving unit with glass shelves. (Design: Justin Meath Baker.)

below Simple metal loops for towels, clothes and bath robe compete with a traditional kitchen chair for practical storage. On baths with sloping sides, a run-around rail is convenient for bath towels. (Design: Philippe Starck, for Duravit.)

right Internal shelves in a deep curving bathroom door create inventive storage boxes for toiletries, books and loofahs. As an alternative, hang a line of bicycle baskets or plastic containers down the middle of a plain door for easy access. A round basin cupboard provides contrasting hideaway storage. (Design: Justin Meath Baker.)

kitchen

ergonomics

With resourceful planning it is possible to design an informal, user-friendly kitchen with a minimum of fuss and expense. Begin with a review of basic appliances and storage requirements. Draw a map or plan of your existing kitchen, plot any changes or additions on paper and re-use or reorganize anything you can. A few simple adjustments can make all the difference to day-to-day efficiency and practicality.

above Hanging wall cupboards are the main feature of this food preparation area. Pull-out drawers make pans and utensils easily accessible. (Design: Rick Baker.)

below A contemporary stainless steel rail in this Japanese kitchen echoes the style of a traditional American Shaker design and provides good eye-level storage.

above Making the most of available light and space under a roof, everything is close to hand in this kitchen. Wheeled units pull out to provide extra surfaces for food preparation. (Design: Justin Meath Baker.)

above Inexpensive zinc sheets fixed with glue and upholstery pins transform basic MDF cupboards. Bright paintwork inside the cupboards, and hand-crafted handles, complete an inspiring make-over. (Design: Justin Meath Baker.)

right In this New York loft, open shelving holds pans, china and glassware, while a row of cupboards underneath provide good-looking storage for kitchen basics. Specialist utensils and equipment are stacked neatly under walk-around tables.

A new relaxation about food preparation, a preference for sharing informal meals in the kitchen with family and friends and a demand for simple environments signal a change in kitchen design and storage style. This keep-it-simple approach adapts easily to any style. So work within an existing architectural framework, apply simple ergonomics and update any kitchen to a functional and welcoming space.

Before you go ahead with a major reorganization, run a quick check on all equipment, utensils and tableware. Divide everything into essential and non-essential items. Use this opportunity to remove any duplicates or extinct items. Why keep identical cheese graters or a rusty wok? Be realistic about storage options. Set a budget and invest in workable solutions that fit all individual requirements. There is no point buying an expensive good-looking system with inadequate storage space. Also, it is important to avoid overcrowding – for safety reasons and efficiency.

left In this dynamic conversion of a 19th-century workshop, a steel bar full of hanging pans and utensils ensures that all essential cooking items are close at hand.

For an efficient kitchen, begin with the position of basic appliances. Provide storage for cookware and tableware within an arm's span of key work stations and activity areas – so, store pots and pans next to a cooking appliance and knives and chopping board next to a work surface. Store tableware next to a sink, dishwasher or table.

Storage possibilities are limitless, ranging from an informal combination of freestanding units, open shelving and hanging racks to a system of built-in units. The key factor in choosing effort-saving solutions is proximity. A drawer under a cooking appliance for pots and pans, pull-out baskets for food storage next to a work surface, or a wall rack beside a sink for clean china and glassware, all provide simple storage and upgrade kitchen efficiency. In a one-wall line-up with all appliances and storage together, the big issue is space-saving flexible storage. Compact options include pull-out shelf racks for food, deep drawers for cookware and tableware, a hanging rack for pots and pans, and a wheel-out unit or trolley with extra work surface and shelves underneath. Any remaining space is free for a table and chairs and general living space.

above A wooden wall slides across to enclose the kitchen, leaving the fridge/freezer in the dining area. Behind panels, this appliance is camouflaged in its new setting. (Architects: Munkenbeck + Marshall.)

left Plain, functional and well put together, this kitchen in an open-plan New York apartment illustrates the fine art of low-key storage.

right Basic white cupboards provide floor-level storage that is ideal for heavy items such as cleaning equipment and saucepans, as well as creating a strong base for a joint worktop and kitchen table.

on display

Matter-of-fact storage solutions – from rustic baskets and jam jars to on-view collections of utensils or everyday foodstuffs – can add vitality and colour to functional catering environments. Simple details such as a line of cooking oils or preserves on a stainless steel shelf or a stack of favourite mixing bowls on a plain worktop will enliven any space. Open kitchen storage, with important items within easy reach, is perfect for the busy cook.

left In this compact country kitchen a simple shelf, plastic plate rack and swivel tea towel rail, allows easy access.

below Criss-cross stainless steel shelves with open brackets take up less space than conventional wooden versions. (Shelves from Slingsby.)

above Economy of effort is often a result of having essential utensils close at hand. This rustic cutlery box is perfect for the middle of the table for everyday meals.

right A stainless steel tray presents espresso cups at the dining table and also acts as a portable makeshift draining board when lined with paper towels.

A kitchen with its workings and contents on view is a welcoming place and, crucially, everything is highly accessible. Typically it might include basic utensils lodged in ceramic pots, rush baskets filled with fresh vegetables, fruit and eggs, jars of preserves on display on shelves and orderly stacks of cooking pots and bowls on a workbench or table. Perhaps as a backlash to laboratory-type kitchens, this fine tradition of presenting a visual index of essentials and good things in store is back in favour. In moderation, and with twists to update this look, open storage translates well to even minimalist-style kitchens.

Simplicity is the key. Avoid the confusion and chaos of taking everything you have out of the pantry and into the open. Instead, you should include only items in frequent use. Bear in mind that accessibility is as crucial as the visual effect. There is little point storing jam jars three-deep on a shelf, or putting your favourite salad bowl under a stack of heavy cookware so it is difficult to remove.

left An out-of-service Dualit toaster is given shelf space as a store for saucepan lids, while a galvanized bucket from a hardware store acts as a practical and generous utensil container.

An "open" kitchen can present many opportunities for creative storage ideas. Kitchen utensils can be stored in tool boxes, or even something as basic as a tin bucket or a terracotta plant pot. By pooling together odds and ends, clutter can be eliminated. A white jug with a selection of favourite wooden implements or an oriental basket or steamer holding a jumble of cooking oils, spice jars and herbs in place next to a hob looks efficient and hardworking.

Kitchens with an emphasis on display are ideal for busy cooks who need to have everything conveniently at hand. For unusual ad hoc storage solutions, choose whatever items fit the environment. A sudden contrast – perhaps an African basket in a marble and stainless-steel kitchen – will look over-exotic. In general, resourceful yet compatible storage works best: Provençal storage jars and creamware jugs for rustics, white ceramics and maple baskets for purists, and metal beakers or glass tank vases for modernists.

left Good accessibility is the feature of this kitchen storage solution. Equipment for food preparation or cooking is neatly stacked and clearly in view. This is no-fuss storage for people who like to cook.

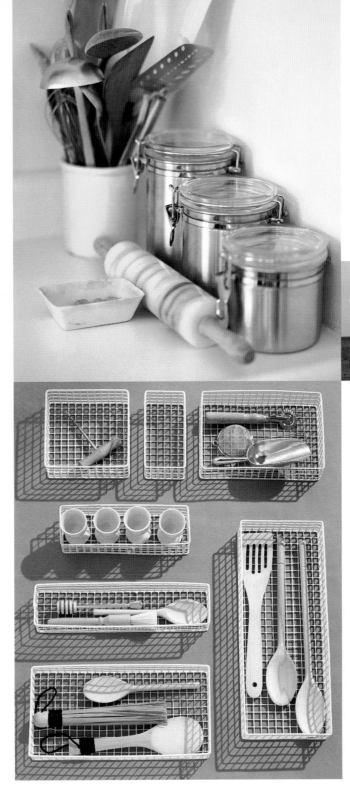

left An orderly line of stainless steel and glass jars in different sizes provides convenient storage for everyday essentials including teabags, coffee and sugar.

below A fold-away two-tier plate rack in stainless steel and wood drains and stores china, glasses and cutlery.

left Individual lift-out containers inside kitchen drawers separate different types of utensils and prevent the usual jumble of everything thrown together.

below A mobile work surface with wide drawer, towel rails and adjustable shelves is ideal for wheeling into action when needed, then storing out of the way.

above A stainless steel rack above a work surface. With a mosaic tile splashback below, it is ideal for draining as well as storing plates.

below Stainless steel bars give this modern kitchen a professional catering look: convenient for drainage, quick access and for hooking up pots and pans.

left This is functional yet decorative storage. Secure a firm fixing for butcher's hooks in a timber beam or wooden rail and hook up kitchen utensils and earthenware pots.

right A series of parallel steel rods fitted with hooks provide compact storage for saucepans and utensils. (Architects: Solveig Fernlund and Neil Logan.)

lofty
i d e a s

A simple hook can have a big impact upon the general efficiency of a kitchen – in a way that expensive storage solutions and kitchen designs often do not. Everyday utensils and pots hanging within easy reach of a cooking surface aid efficiency and symbolize a cook at work. Hooks and hanging rails provide logical and functional no-fuss storage for effective kitchens.

Hooks and hanging rails, with a jumble of pots and utensils, offer an anti-order storage option. There are no cupboard doors to open or slide out of the way, and no place for artifice or to display items that collect dust – just sensible storage for everyday equipment.

Before you opt for this level of exposure, lay out everything you plan to hang up. Divide up and position items according to function around the kitchen; for example, deposit mugs by the kettle and pans and utensils by the cooker. Take a look at how much there is to hang (allow for a few acquisitions over time) and work out where everything can go.

Use hooks, hanging rails or frames. Simple hooks work well for small items such as earthenware jugs or aprons and tea towels. Rails and frames are ideal for pans and utensils. A good fixing to a wall or beam is critical, especially if you plan to hang everything with a handle from a single steel rail. Hanging frames, perhaps above a work surface, will distribute weight evenly.

left A luggage rack from a train provides unusual and versatile storage for kitchen utensils. With scope to hook up baskets for extra storage, it makes a striking display.

left A washing machine, tumble drier, fridge, freezer and pull-out food racks form a precise geometric arrangement in this kitchen. Swing-open doors provide easy access to laundry appliances and conceal control panels. (Architect: Gunnar Orefelt.)

right Opaque perspex door panels create a seamless line from standard kitchen units and basic appliances. A continuous stainless steel worktop and mosaic splashback complete the architectural simplicity of the scheme. (Architects: Munkenbeck + Marshall.)

below A spacious drawer underneath a stainless steel oven and hob provides ample storage for roasting tins, baking trays and large chopping boards. The wood-veneer finish on the drawer co-ordinates with kitchen cupboards throughout.

appliances

Raw kitchen appliances can look out of place within a co-ordinating kitchen, so storage is a critical factor. Replace or fix fascia panels onto appliance doors to conceal standard fittings and unify a design scheme. If possible, store laundry appliances in a separate area, or slot them into standard kitchen unit frames with swing-open doors to reduce noise levels and hide control panels. Check ventilation and plumbing requirements before committing to any major changes.

utility room

right This compact canvas and metal frame laundry bin for bedrooms and bathrooms is a welcome update on conventional Alibaba baskets.

left The luxury and convenience of a traditional built-in storage cupboard is shown off in a bathroom of a London townhouse. Narrow shelves inside provide ample space for towels, linen and essential supplies. (Design: Eliza Cairns.)

cleaning and
laundry

Without labour-saving ideas and good storage solutions, cleaning and laundry can become a chore. Simple ideas, like storing washing powder on a shelf directly above a washing machine and sorting cleaning equipment into individual buckets for particular cleaning tasks, can minimize effort and save time. Flexible options such as folding laundry bins and pull-up ceiling racks provide instant storage or back-up for seasonal changes. Likewise, pull-out and wheel-around kitchen units with shelves for cleaning equipment or an ironing board on a permanent pull-down wall fixing, provide flexible storage to increase efficiency and convenience.

above In this compact utility area all the essentials are stored within easy reach. Catering tins hold washing powders and soaps, while buckets are housed under the sink.

right Wheel out this professional metal bin on washdays for storing substantial laundry bundles. It is also useful for transporting cleaning equipment. (From Slingsby.)

above This foldaway lightweight laundry bin with removable stringmesh bag and wheels is ideal for collecting and storing washing or general household items. (From Slingsby.)

right A sculptural shopping trolley is perfectly compatible with the sandblasted glass partitions and industrial fittings in this schoolhouse conversion. Its graphic profile compensates for its basic function of storing lavatory supplies.

below Once a clothing locker in a New York public swimming bath, this wire basket is convenient for storing spare candles and specialist cleaning equipment for silverware. Use any basket or container in this way.

right The front of this mobile kitchen unit flips down to reveal a plastic waste bucket. Inside, a network of different shelves provide specific storage for cleaning cloths, tin foil and food storage bags. (Design: Justin Meath Baker.)

For the storage of large-scale cleaning and laundry equipment, like vacuum cleaners and ironing boards, nominate a single cupboard if you can, and keep everything in one place for convenience. Arrange equipment so that heavy items are directly on the floor and nearest the door – as this will save unnecessary lifting. For cylinder cleaners, remove the plastic hose and hang it over a nail or hook to save space. Brooms and mops can be hung on the inside of the cupboard door. Buy the sort that have a handle with holes in the top or drill a hole and make a loop of string or tape to hook onto wall fixings.

Buckets are ideal storage for cleaning cloths, liquid sprays and polish. Store everything in one bucket and simply take it with you on your chores. As well as being portable, buckets can hang out of the way or stack on top of each other to save space. Collect laundry in mobile foldaway containers or line conventional laundry bins with muslin sacks and simply remove the sack with the laundry on wash-days.

right An inexpensive plastic bin with handle is an artful companion for heavy-duty cleaning. Replace the lid for practical permanent storage for cleaning cloths, bin liners and liquid sprays.

home office

right Multi-drawer units such as this wire system provide storage for essential office items. Invent a quick-search system by attaching photographs of what is inside on the front of each drawer.

left Good-sized baskets in metal make ideal portable storage bins for paperwork or files. Look out for ex-industrial metal trays in office warehouse sales or seek out exotic grocery boxes.

pen and
paper

below Library and department store style are combined in these traditional storage items. Such pieces are ideal for modern home offices.

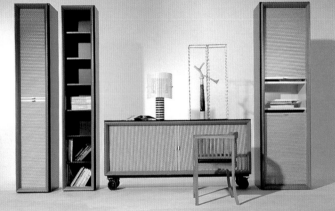

right A rustic Mexican table, sculptural metal stools, an original clothes locker from a public swimming bath and metal jars for storing pens and pencils provide stylish basics for a daytime office area at one end of this apartment.

above Precision building-block units for equipment and information storage co-ordinate to individual specifications to provide flexible add-on home office storage.

right In any office in a domestic environment, special human elements, like this collection of oriental baskets for storing pencils and rubber bands, will serve to offset work-like precision and conformity.

Working from home is now a viable empowering option for many people. The rapid expansion in communication networks, inexpensive computer systems and new thinking about how, where and when we work, all contribute to this change. The setting up of an office in the home brings with it unique problems, but with imaginative storage it can be achieved successfully – even within the smallest of spaces. Organization with flexibility is the key to success.

If you opt to work from home, aim to take over a whole room and set it up as a welcoming, ready-to-use environment. There is no reason for this space to look like a conventional office, and as it is self-contained you will not be restricted to fitting in with design decisions elsewhere in the house. However, it is possible that you will have to use an area within an established room for your home office. The main consideration with dual-function environments is how to organize space and store equipment without compromising work or living activities.

Apart from essential investments like excellent seating, a solid work surface, good basic equipment and lighting, this is an ideal opportunity to invest in creative storage solutions. Mix industrial shelving with metal cupboards and mobile drawer units in low-key industrial style; perhaps opt for a traditional oak desk with library shelves and consider commissioning a custom-built system of storage units and work surface or choose specialist fittings from contract suppliers.

right In a New York apartment, a modernist red table effectively frames and diffuses the raw industrial feel of an assertive line-up of heavy-duty metal filing cabinets. (Design: C.I.T.E.)

Whether your idea of an essential work space is a computer terminal with fax, answerphone and coffee machine, or a plain table with a sheet of paper and a pencil, ample storage will prevent an office from taking over a domestic set-up.

Open-plan interiors offer many possibilities for delineating office space. Partitions, screens or storage units can be used to divide working and living areas. For conventional dual-function areas (a kitchen table, bedroom alcove or hallway) re-organize existing storage or introduce mobile storage units. Alternatively, choose new units with ample storage potential in a style that is in keeping with existing surroundings. A metal front-opening travel trunk, Shaker-style kitchen cabinet or modular wall units all provide functional options and fit in with contemporary interiors. For fax machines, small printers and photocopiers, sturdy trolleys in metal, plastic or wood provide a practical option. The simpler the storage solution, the quicker the transition from work space to living space, and vice versa.

above In an open-plan New York apartment an antique desk and a modern plastic trolley provide ample storage and work space.

left Good organization and under-desk storage limits the impact of essential computer equipment and office paperwork upon living space.

right Mobile storage units can be wheeled in and out to screen office activities during working hours. (Mobile unit from Driade.)

right Built in a prime position in good light, this flip-down desk makes clever use of space. Cupboards below and on either side provide ample storage for books, files and fax machine.

small-scale storage

small-scale
storage

Finding storage solutions for small-scale essentials will revolutionize the way you live with a new sense of order. Avoid convention and use kitchen items in bathrooms for storing sponges, soaps and body brushes; introduce office surplus into bedrooms for socks, underwear and accessories; and garden pots into kitchens to store stainless steel and wooden utensils. Explore the hidden possibilities of plastic boxes as drawer dividers and baskets inside cupboards for extra efficiency and a welcome sense of space. They can provide storage that is decorative and personal.

above A metal basket, containing kitchen sink clutter such as washing-up brushes, cloths and liquids, acts as a convenient sink-tidy. Use a separate basket for storing clean cutlery or vegetable brushes.

right Any size or shape of rustic basket provides ideal storage in a country-style interior. Hang them from simple nails or hooks in kitchens, bathrooms or hallways for household essentials.

left An inexpensive oriental basket, like this Chinese vegetable steamer, available from specialist supermarkets or kitchen suppliers, can easily be upgraded to become a decorative storage item.

above Store everyday kitchen utensils in simple open baskets for order and accessibility. Teaspoons can sit alongside a kettle, while wooden spoons or spatulas can sit next to a cooking surface.

left Sweep up any random collections of holiday photographs, household bills, documents or CDs in multi-use cardboard and metal storage boxes. They are ideal for visible stacks on tables or on open shelving systems, inside wardrobes or under beds. (Boxes from Muji.)

right Pull-out boxes for sewing kits or baskets for knitting provide lightweight portable storage. Use containers with handles and devise an easy-reference labelling system – perhaps plastic bags stuck to the front with a sample of the contents.

left Metal or plastic lunch boxes make versatile and protective storage for special interest items such as camera equipment or art materials. For alternative hard-wearing storage containers, visit office suppliers for cash boxes, mini-safes and filing boxes.

Boxes eliminate the visual clutter of collections of small-scale items and provide efficient storage solutions for everyday require-ments, from a stack of CDs to household documents. Use plastic or cardboard open boxes for organizing the inside of cupboards; they are ideal for piles of T-shirts, tablelinen or toys. Store boxes along the bottom of a cupboard or on basic shelving for easy access. For dust-free storage for fragile clothing, computer discs or any paraphernalia not in everyday circulation, use boxes with lids.

As a low-cost do-it-yourself storage system, wall-mount a series of parallel shelves to provide a basic framework. Then slot in rows of boxes within the shelves. Fix optional side panels for extra definition or construct a free-standing frame on wheels. Either way, keep the top shelf clear for opening and sorting individual boxes. Devise a quick-reference labelling scheme, perhaps luggage tags, coloured adhesive labels, letters of the alphabet or numbers. Alternatively, use a selection of different or semi-transparent plastic boxes so that you can see the individual contents at a glance.

Although there is a wide selection of specialist products and designs to match small-scale storage requirements for bathrooms, it is worth looking beyond the conventional choices and putting together an eclectic mixture of essentials with wit and originality.

Stick to basics if you want a contemporary style. Plain white china mugs, jugs and bowls, glass tumblers and metal beakers provide low-cost storage for toothbrushes, natural sponges and soaps. Often, a simple change of environment for familiar household objects is sufficient to create a new look.

For cosmetics and cotton wool, use transparent pencil cases, food jars with snap-lids and plastic food boxes. Semi-transparent or opaque storage items will look good in bathrooms. Use glass flower vases for body brushes and loofahs and frosty dessert dishes for soaps. Convert bubble-glass cooking oil jars and miniature spice jars into decorative storage for lotions and home-made aromatic bath oils.

left Basic white china, glass and metal containers from the kitchen can be moved to the bathroom for simple storage. Add a favourite decorative piece to enliven and personalize a basic line-up.

right Bring decorative garden urns and plant pots indoors for imaginative storage solutions. Also, mix together wire boxes, plant containers and stone pots.

above Inexpensive terracotta pots and earthenware storage jars work well with period fittings and add colour and texture to country-style bathrooms.

right Empty jam jars or French storage jars with snap-lids provide inexpensive solutions for keeping together essential odds and ends such as pencils, rubber bands, stamps and paper clips.

Re-invent, re-cycle and re-use familiar household items as alternative storage solutions. For example, transfer talcum powder to a sugar shaker for easy sprinkling, keep household receipts, take-away menus and timetables on an office-surplus clipboard and hang up on the back of a cupboard door, and re-use cardboard shoe boxes for photographs or stationery.

Recycle jam jars, plastic ice-cream boxes and biscuit tins for convenient airtight food storage. Both hardware stores and office suppliers are a good source for a mass of ad hoc storage items. Use expandable toolboxes for toiletries, cosmetics or sewing kit, or convert perspex mini drawer-systems, originally for screws and nails, for cotton tips, tweezers and nail scissors. Similarly, colourful petty cash boxes or safes are ideal as jewellery boxes; metal or plastic paper trays work well as storage for belts and scarves, and waste paper baskets are useful for keeping magazines and newspapers in order in living environments.

right For low-cost storage, re-cycle food cans for pens and pencils, fabric swatches or darning wools. Use a can opener to remove any sharp edges and always wash cans thoroughly.

below Stacks of colourful rustic boxes provide decorative storage in both country-style and contemporary interiors.

right The simplicity and honesty of Shaker boxes can offset machine-age entertainment equipment in multi-functional living environments.

left Mix and match a collection of ethnic baskets for decorative colour-coded storage on open shelving.

right An ex-swimming costume mannequin is an unusual hanging frame for kitchen mugs. Explore the possibilities of topiary frames in sculptural or animal shapes for a similar decorative display.

Transposing historic or ethnic storage items into contemporary settings can provide new storage possibilities far removed from the original commonplace use.

Historic Shaker boxes with an inherent simplicity, originally made by craftspeople for storing everyday kitchen and workshop items, now look out of place in workaday situations. Antique country boxes, earthenware or stone storage jars, milk jugs and medicine jars, once seen as functional items, are too precious for kitchen or general household items. Use these storage treasures for jewellery, mementos and anything of personal value.

For decorative general storage, look to ethnic basketware and also simple wooden boxes. Often inexpensive yet with fine detailing or craftwork, these are ideal for many practical storage applications. Use colourful African market baskets, originally for carrying fruit and vegetables, to store clothing and magazines, and oriental vegetable steamers or sisal spice baskets as containers for cosmetics and toiletries.

With imagination, many antique items that were not originally designed for the purpose, can also provide decorative storage.

garden and garage

storage
shelters

Garden sheds and garages are areas that require common sense storage solutions. Gardening is a hands-on outdoor activity that begins with a visit to a shed, or possibly a shelf or bin, to stock up with equipment. Apart from a table or worktop for repotting or sharpening tools, a single row of long nails will provide no-fuss storage for hanging spades, rakes and forks. A galvanized bin will prevent fertilisers and plant food from drying out or getting too damp. In sizeable gardens, a wheelbarrow is useful for transporting equipment, while a gardening apron with pockets is handy for compact gardens.

above An outdoor peg rail under the shelter of an overhanging roof provides orderly storage for garden tools, a plant box and wicker basket. A line of basic nails will work as well.

left A slatted wooden shelf on bracket mounts makes a simple, well-drained potting table with space to store various plants and galvanized florist's buckets.

left A traditional wicker gardener's basket, with sturdy handle and tape, stores tools and gardening gloves. With space for plants, seeds or bulbs, it is a practical companion for any gardener.

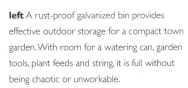

left A rust-proof galvanized bin provides effective outdoor storage for a compact town garden. With room for a watering can, garden tools, plant feeds and string, it is full without being chaotic or unworkable.

In garages, even with a car inside, there is ample storage potential on walls and ceilings. For sports equipment such as skis or bicycles, invest in specialist wall or ceiling brackets available from sports suppliers. Alternatively, for a bicycle, secure a firm wall-fixing for two heavy-duty shelf brackets and support the frame under the crossbar or below the seat and handle bars. For rackets, bats, balls and sports shoes, fix a high-level shelf – a wooden rack on brackets or a series of wooden or metal parallel poles stretching across one wall with occasional brackets underneath for extra support. Hang hooks on the poles for additional storage for gardening implements or sports clothing.

For tools, household maintenance and decorating equipment, metal filing cabinets with good-sized drawers for tins of paint and electrical tools are in keeping with the work-a-day look of a garage environment. Plastic boxes and chipboard shelves or self-assembly units work well for a typical mix of different-sized tools and essentials.

left A self-assembly modular unit, with optional doors and shelf components, stores tools and equipment and provides a strong base for a simple work table. (Cubekit from Cubestore.)

above Ex-household or broken items often resurface in tool sheds or garages as ad hoc storage solutions. This split cutlery tray, in use as a decorator's store for paint brushes and varnish, is a typical example.

right Colourful plastic bottle crates brighten up a garage, cellar, modern kitchen or understairs area. Ideal for wine, water or soft drinks, they can be stacked to save space. (Jasper Morrison rack.)

above For household maintenance or professional cleaning, this mobile unit offers a waste bin and plastic waistcoat. (Bucket from Slingsby.)

left Under-sink pull-out plastic storage bins for domestic waste make recycling a practical option. Each bin is split in half and lifts out separately for depositing in an outdoor domestic recycling bin, compost heap, or recycling bank. The lid lifts or seals automatically when the unit moves in or out. (Recycling bin by Goldreif.)

below For outdoor use, this multi-purpose skip on wheels provides ample storage space for recycling newspapers, tins or bottles. (Container from Slingsby.)

recycling

An active interest in recycling domestic waste requires specific storage. This includes a selection of individual or split bins with lids for every kind of waste product – from bottles and vegetable matter to paper and aluminium tins. If there is space under the kitchen sink or on the floor of a kitchen cupboard, a line of simple plastic buckets with lids will work as well as any specialist storage item. Cardboard boxes from a supermarket are useful for collecting newspapers.

directory

Check with the following suppliers and retailers for any additional information about nationwide stockists, mail order, export and overseas agents or stockists.

GREAT BRITAIN

Aero
96 Westbourne Grove
London
W2 5RT
tel 0171 221 1950
fax 0171 221 2555

Ron Arad
62 Chalk Farm Road
London
NW1 8AN
tel 0171 284 4963
fax 0171 379 0499

Aram
3 Kean Street
London
WC2 4AT
tel 0171 240 3933

Arc Linea
164 Brompton Road
Knightsbridge
London SW3 1HW
tel 0171 581 2271
fax 0171 581 7912

Atrium
Centrepoint
22-24 St Giles High Street
London
WC2H 8LN
tel 0171 379 7288
fax 0171 240 2080

Rick Baker
(Enquiries)
Workshop
F2 Cross Lane
London
N8 7SA
tel 0181 340 2020
fax 0181 341 1620

Bulthaup
37 Wigmore
London
W1H 9LD
tel 0171 495 3663
fax 0171 495 0139

Century Design
68 Marylebone High Street
London
W1M 3AQ
tel 0171 487 5100

Coexistence
288 Upper Street
London
N1 2TZ
tel 0171 354 8817
fax 0171 354 9610

The Conran Shop
Michelin House
81 Fulham Road
London
SW3 6RD
tel 0171 589 7401
fax 0171 823 7015

C. P. Hart
Newnham Terrace
Hercules Road
London
SE1 7DR
tel 0171 902 1000
fax 0171 902 1001

Cubestore
(Enquiries)
London Road Industrial Estate
Brandon
Suffolk IP27 0ND
tel 0181 994 6016

Divertimenti
139 Fulham Road
London
SW3 6SD
0171 581 8065
Customer mail order:
tel 0171 386 9911

**The English Garden
Collection**
P O Box 1030
Langley
Slough
Berkshire
SL3 8BX
Catalogue request line:
tel 0800 103 000

The Futon Company
169 Tottenham Court Road
London
W1P 9LH
tel 0171 636 9984

Mark Gabbertas
(Enquiries)
Oblique Workshops
Stamford Works
Gillett Street
London N16 8JH
tel 0171 275 7495/
0171 381 1847

General Trading Company
144 Sloane Street
London SW1X 9BL
tel 0171 730 0411
fax 0171 823 4624

Goldreif Kitchens
(Enquiries)
Silbury Court
368 Silbury Boulevard
Central Milton Keynes
MK9 2AF
tel 01908 606886
fax 01908 606958

Habitat
196 Tottenham Court Road
London
W1P 9LD
Customer Services:
tel 0645 334433

Nick Hill
(Enquiries)
85 Southbroom Road
Devizes
Wiltshire SN10 1LX
tel 01380 723294

The Holding Company
243-245 Kings Road
London SW3 5EL
tel 0171 352 1600
fax 0171 352 7495

Ikea
2 Drury Way
North Circular Road
London
NW10 0TH
Customer services:
tel 0181 208 5600

Jam
(Enquiries)
7 Seymour House
Churchway
London
NW1 1LR
tel 0171 916 1478

Janie Jackson
tel 0171 912 0882

Jinan Gallery
17 Golden Square
London
W1R 4JB
tel 0171 434 3464
fax 0171 434 3463

Justin Meath Baker
Baker Nevile Associates
tel 0171 403 3137

Ligne Roset
(Enquiries)
95A High Street
Great Missenden
Buckinghamshire
HP16 0AL
tel 01494 865001

Missing Link
52 Rectory Square
London
E1 3NG
tel 0171 790 5144

Andrew Mortada
tel 0171 739 3027

Muji
26 Great Marlborough Street
London
W1V 1HL
tel 0171 494 1197
fax 0171 494 1193

**Munkenbeck + Marshall
Architects**
3 Pine Street
London
EC1R 0JH
tel 0171 833 1407
fax 0171 837 5416

Oggetti
133 & 143 Fulham Road
London
SW3 6RT
tel 0171 581 8088/9808
fax 0171 581 9652

Gunnar Orefelt
Orefelt Associates
4 Portobello Studios
5 Haydens Place
London
W11 1LY
tel 0171 243 3181
fax 0171 792 1126

Purves & Purves
80–81 & 83
Tottenham Court Road
London
W1P 9HD
tel 0171 580 8223

Charles Rutherfoord
tel 0171 627 0182
fax 0171 720 0799

SCP
135–139 Curtain Road
London
EC2A 3BX
tel 0171 739 1869
fax 0171 729 4224

The Shaker Shop
25 Harcourt Street
London
W1 1DT
tel 0171 724 7672
fax 0171 724 6640
Mail order enquiries:
0171 724 7672

Siematic Mobelweke UK
(Enquiries)
Osprey House
Rookery Court
Primett Road
Stevenage
SG1 3EE
tel 01438 369251
fax 01438 368920

H C Slingsby
(Head office and export)
Preston Street
Bradford
BD7 1JF
tel 01274 721591
fax 01274 723044

The Source
10 Harbour Parade
West Quay
Southampton
SO15 1BA
tel 01703 336141

**Stickland Coombe
Architecture**
tel 0171 924 1699

Malcolm Temple
(Enquiries)
36 Trebovir Road
London
SW5 9NJ
tel 0171 373 6122

Twentieth Century Design
274 Upper Street
Islington
London
N1 2UA
tel 0171 288 1996

Viaduct
1-10 Summer's Street
London
EC1R 5BD
tel 0171 278 8456
fax 0171 278 2844

Vitra
13 Grosvenor Street
London
W1X 9FB
tel 0171 408 1122
fax 0171 499 1967

David Wainwright
61-63 Portobello Road
London
W11 3DB
tel 0171 727 0707

Water Monopoly
16-18 Lonsdale Road
London NW6 6RD
tel 0171 624 2636
fax 0171 624 2631

UNITED STATES

Aero
132 Spring Street
New York
NY 10012
tel 212 966 1500

C.I.T.E.
100 Wooster Street
New York
NY 10012
tel 212 431 7272
fax 212 226 6507

Crate & Barrel
650 Madison Avenue
New York
NY 10022
tel 212 308 0011

Dialogica
484 Broome Street
New York
NY 10013
tel 212 966 1934
fax 212 966 2870

**Fernlund & Logan
Architects**
135 Rivington Street
New York
NY 10002
tel 212 473 7387
fax 212 674 9164

Tricia Foley
New York
tel 212 348 0074
fax 212 423 9146

Gansevoort Gallery
72 Gansevoort Street
New York
NY 10014
tel 212 633 0555
fax 212 633 1808

Hold Everything
P O Box 7807
San Francisco
CA 94120-7807
tel 1-800 421 2264
Customer Services:
tel 1-800 421 2285

**Ligne Roset (USA)
Corporation**
New York Design Centre
200 Lexington Avenue
New York
NY 10016
tel 212 685 2238

Modern Age
102 Wooster Street
New York
NY 10012
tel 212 966 0669
fax 212 966 4167

Modernica
7366 Beverly Boulevard
Los Angeles
California 90036
tel 213 933 0383
fax 213 933 0159

Parallel Design
430 West 14th Street
Suite 408
New York
NY 10014
tel 212 989 4959
fax 212 989 4977

Annabelle Selldorf
Selldorf Architects
62 White Street
New York
NY 10013
tel 212 219 9571
fax 212 941 6362

Vicente Wolf Associates
333 West 39th Street
New York
NY 10018
tel 212 465 0590
fax 212 465 0639

EUROPE

Arc Linea Arredamenti Spa
(Enquiries)
Via Pasubio 50
36030 Caldogno
Vicenza
Italy
tel (0444) 39411
fax (0444) 394262

Bieffeplast
Via Pelosa 78
35030 Caselle di Selvezzano
Padova
Italy
tel (0039) 49 8730111
fax (0039) 49 635323

The Conran Shop
117 Rue du Bac
75007 Paris
France
tel (00331) 42 84 1001
fax (00331) 42 84 2975

Fiam Italia Spa
Via Ancona 1/b
61010 Tavullia
Italy
tel (0039) 721 20 1346
fax (0039) 721 20 2432

Goldreif
Mobelfabrik GmbH & Co
Meerbrede 4
32107 Bad Salzuflen
Germany
tel (0049) 52 21 7710

Habitat
Wagram
35 Avenue de Wagram
75017 Paris
France
tel (00331) 47 66 2552

Kartell
Via Delle Industrie 1
20082 Noviglio
Milan
Italy
tel (0039) 2 900 121
fax (0039) 2 905 3316

Ligne Roset S.A
(Enquiries)
01470 Serriéres de Briord
Ain
France
tel (0033) 47 43 61700

OF SPECIAL NOTE

Stephen Mack
Stephen P. Mack Associates
Chase Hill Farm
Ashaway
Rhode Island
02804
tel 401-377-8041
Stephen Mack is a nationally
renowned architectural and
interior designer and expert in
the restoration and
reconstruction of 17th- and
18th-century structures and their
environs.

projects

storage
boxes

Simple shoe boxes can make good-looking
storage for home office items, such as
notebooks and envelopes. This project
explains how to cover and line a shoe box
with identical fabric, although you can use
fabric offcuts and mix and match different
designs. Cotton, linen or felt are ideal fabrics.
If you want to use thicker fabric, do not line
the box as this will make it too bulky for the
lid. Check that the shoe box is in good repair
before you begin, and fix any internal flaps
with glue, staples or tape.

you will need:

⅓m/⅓yd of fabric

Shoe box

Pencil or marker

Ruler, straight edge or set square

Scissors

Sticky tape, heavy book or drawing pins

Tape measure

Sheet of paper or newspaper

*Rubber- or water-based glue (which will not stain or
show through fabric; if using felt you can use double-
sided sticky tape instead of glue)*

Radiator roller or art roller (optional)

Fraystop (optional)

*Ribbon or braid to wrap around the outside of the lid
(optional)*

*Label of some kind – possibly a photograph or plastic
bag showing a sample of the box's contents (optional)*

❶ Press the fabric flat with an iron and check
that it is cut straight (at right angles) in the
direction of the grain. Line up with the table, ruler,
set square or shoe box to check. If necessary, you
may have to trim the sides.

❷ Lay out the fabric on a work table or cutting board.
Using sticky tape (or alternatively, a heavy book or drawing
pins), fix the fabric to the table so that it remains flat.
Remove the lid from the shoe box and put it to one side.

❸ Cut two pieces of fabric: one piece of fabric that
will cover the outside base and ends (short sides) of
the shoe box, inside and out; the other piece
of fabric will cover the inside base and long sides of
the shoe box, inside and out. You can use the shoe
box to mark out a template directly onto the fabric
(see step 4). Alternatively, you can use a tape measure
to measure the size of the box and mark out the fabric, or
mark out a template on a sheet of paper or newspaper
and cut the fabric to the size of the paper.

4 To measure the first piece, tip the shoe box on one side and line up the outside edges with the edges of fabric.

5 Mark the width of the box on the fabric with a pencil dot; flip the box along the fabric onto its base and opposite side. Use light pencil dots to mark the outside points. This amount of fabric will cover the outside of the box.

6 To add enough fabric to line the two inside ends, move the box along the fabric to measure two more end pieces. Mark with pencil dots.

7 Now join all of the outer dots with a faint pencil line. Cut out the fabric. Attach this wide piece of fabric to the box first.

8 Apply a thin layer of glue on one outside long side of the box, and smooth the fabric over it. One end of the fabric should be in line with the base of the box.

9 Read the instructions on the glue packet – you may have to wait a while for the glue to dry. Now sit the box upright so that you can see into the shoe box. The fabric is going to line the inside of the box and the opposite outer side, so work with the bulk of the fabric toward you.

10 Apply glue to the first inner long side and smooth the fabric firmly, working from the middle of the cut edge of the fabric to the outside edges of the box and toward you. You may find that a radiator or art roller is useful. Wipe away any excess glue if it oozes out from the sides, and take care not to get glue on the right side of the fabric.

11 Apply glue to the base and second inner long side and fix the fabric smoothly and firmly. The fabric should fit neatly into the corners of the box. If you have cut more than you need, apply extra glue along the edges of the wrong side of the fabric and fix firmly to the box. Fix the last bit of fabric to the final outer long side, opposite to the side where you began.

12 To cut the second piece of fabric, repeat the process but work along the length of the box instead of the width. Begin by sitting the box on one end.

13 Glue the fabric to the inside end of the shoe box. Work around the outside of the box, the base and finish on the opposite inside end.

14 For the lid, sit the top of the lid face down on the fabric. Mark the size with pencil dots at each corner. Join the dots with a ruler and cut out. Unless you are using felt, apply fraystop to the fabric edges before gluing.

15 Fix the fabric to the lid top with glue, taking care to fix all of the edges and corners. To finish the sides of the lid, cut a strip of fabric the length of all four sides (or use ribbon) and fix to the lid with glue.

16 For labelling, you could use index cards, luggage tags or even a snapshot of what is inside. Better still, make your own visual index with sample contents in a transparent bag on the front of each box.

cutlery
roll

A cutlery roll is a traditional way to store precious cutlery in individual pockets, free from dust and possible damage from scratching. Whether you have contemporary stainless steel cutlery or more formal silver plate or silver ware, each roll makes a neat and easy parcel to store in a cupboard or drawer. It is also a convenient way to carry cutlery to the table. If you have an extensive collection of cutlery for big gatherings yet use the same cutlery for everyday meals, store the bulk of the collection in individual rolls of knives and spoons and make a single roll for everyday place settings. If you want to keep all cutlery pieces in circulation, swap the contents of the everyday roll from time to time. Alternatively, make individual cutlery rolls for different members of the family — each one a different colour.

you will need:

Soft tea towel or tea towel-sized piece of felt

Pins

Ruler

Pencil (or tailor's chalk)

Sewing machine or needle and thread

Approximately 60cm/23½in of tape or ribbon, or 2 x 30cm/11¾in lengths

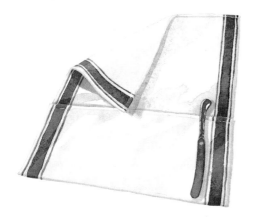

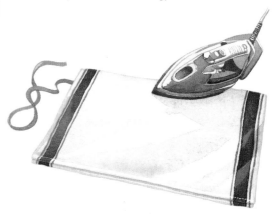

6 Stitch the outside seams and along the pencil lines or rows of pins with a good fixing or knot at the top of each of the seams. Remove the pins. (Tack and remove the pins for machine-stitching.)

1 Lay out the tea towel right side down and turn back approximately one-third of the length. Lay an item of cutlery on the turn-back to check that it is the right size to cover most of the handle. If you are mixing items of cutlery in the same roll, check each item of cutlery for size on the turn-back. Expose enough of each handle to make the item easy to remove.

3 Continue along the roll, marking pockets with a line of pins. If you are mixing items of cutlery in the same roll, measure each pocket with the relevant pieces of cutlery; spoons require wider pockets than knives.

4 With identical items, save time by inserting an item of cutlery, marking the width of the pocket and marking the remaining pockets with a ruler and pencil to the same width.

7 Insert the longest item of cutlery and fold down the top of the tea towel to cover the pockets. Mark the fold line with a pin, remove the cutlery and press the top fold with an iron. This will help the top fold to lie flat on top of the cutlery, hold its shape and stay in place when rolled. For extra definition, machine-stitch a permanent crease along this fold.

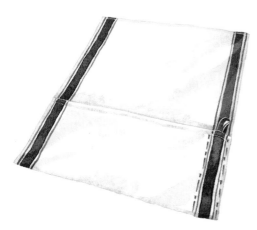

2 Once you have established the correct size of the turn-back, pin to secure on either side. Slip the item of cutlery inside the folded section of the tea towel, and pin either side of the item to make a snug pocket.

5 Before you tack and stitch along each pencil line or row of pins, fold a length of ribbon in half lengthways and insert the fold of the ribbon into one of the side seams near the top of the pockets. As the ribbon wraps around the roll to tie and secure the bundle, check that it is on the outside edge when the roll is complete. Insert the ribbon and pin in place.

hanging
rack

A soft hanging pocket is ideal for storing outdoor accessories like hats and scarves in hallways and porches. Make a storage rack by hanging a line of pockets beside or behind the front door on a length of dowel, a painted broom handle or a (thick) bamboo pole suspended between two hooks. Fix two lines of hanging pockets at different levels to suit different members of the family. Hanging pockets at child height is a friendly way to encourage children to store essential items of outdoor clothing in a convenient place – where they know where to find them!

you will need (for one pocket):

Fabric place mat

Pins

12 eyelets and eyelet tool

Woven fabric tape, approximately 3cm/1¼in wide (or similar medium-density ribbon)

Scissors

1m/1yd of string or leather ribbon or cord

Sewing machine or needle and thread

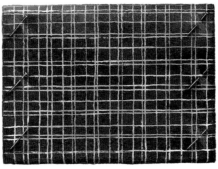

1 Fold the place mat in half, either lengthways or widthways depending on the shape of pocket you wish to make. Make three marks for eyelets along each side using pins. Position the pins evenly, approximately 80–100cm/ 31½–39⅓in apart, and pin front and back.

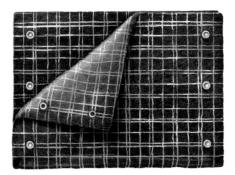

2 Now fix the eyelets to correspond with the pin markers on either side of the fabric. Remove the pins.

3 To fix ribbons or cloth tape to hang the pocket from a pole, cut two strips of identical length to fix either side of the pocket.

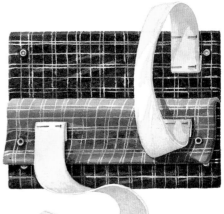

4 Make a loop with each strip on the inside of the pocket, as shown above. Pin in place, and tuck under the ends of tape for a neat finish. Machine- or hand-stitch.

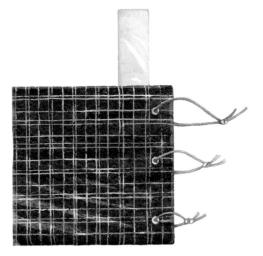

5 For built-in flexibility, tie the side seams with string or leather ribbon. Cut the string in varying lengths, so that the top piece is approximately twice as long as the bottom piece. Loop through the eyelets and knot.

underbed
storage

A low platform on wheels can create valuable extra storage by utilizing the space under the bed to store a wide range of items out of view. For magazines, spare bedlinen and sports shoes use 4 x 50kg/100lb load-bearing castors, one in each corner, and a 15mm/½in depth platform. If you plan to store heavier items, check the load limit for each castor and use heavy-duty castors; choose a material with suitable strength and rigidity for the platform. Perhaps make two or three underbed platforms, accessible from different sides of the bed, and allocate each platform a specific storage function such as camera equipment or household accounts. Store everyday items in frequent use at the front of the platform for easy access.

you will need:

*Chipboard or wooden platform – 15mm/½in depth
(Other dimensions at your discretion – consider the size of bed and the number of platforms required.)*

Pencil

Postcard or small piece of card to improvise a set square; or use a set square or ruler

Castors (4 x 50kg/100lb) and screws to fix

Drill

Screwdriver

Paint, tung oil or varnish (if you plan to decorate or seal the platform)

"D" handle with fixings

1 Lie the platform surface upside down on a solid work table. (As an alternative work surface, protect a dining table with a spare blanket and newspapers.)

2 To mark the position for one castor, square up a postcard in a corner of the platform, keeping the outside edges of the postcard in line with the outside edges of the platform. Draw a light pencil mark around the innermost corner of the postcard. Extend each pencil line by approximately 4 or 5cm/1½ or 2in.

3 Make pencil marks in this way in each corner. Use the pencil markings in each corner of the chipboard or wood platform as a guide to position each castor.

4 Sit the castor snug between the pencil lines. Now mark the innermost screw position; drill a hole in the platform and fix this screw in place.

5 Double-check the alignment of the castor with pencil lines, and mark the remaining screw positions. Drill and fix the screws. Repeat for all castors.

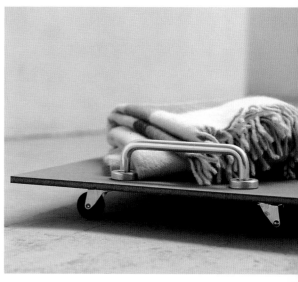

6 Turn the platform over again. If you plan to paint, seal or varnish the wood do so now – before you fix the handle in place. As an alternative to a "D" handle, you may want to make a rope pull. For this you need to drill two holes in the platform and thread thick rope through with a knot at each end on the underside.

7 Fix the "D" handle on whichever end of the platform will be easiest to reach under the bed. For maximum flexibility and accessibility, you may want to fix a handle on each side of the platform.

laundry
bag

A drawstring bag inside a laundry basket is ideal for concealing a mini-mountain of laundry – before or after washing. The bag folds down completely so that laundry can be stacked or sorted easily before it is concealed in the bag. It is useful for storing laundry, out-of-season clothes, spare duvets and pillows, or a mixture of items waiting for the next car-boot sale or charity fair.

you will need:

A firm basket as base, ideally with handles on the side

2½m/2¾yd ticking or fabric (depending on the size of basket)

Scissors

Pencil or tailor's chalk

Long ruler or straight edge

Pins

Sewing machine or needle and thread

3m/3⅓yd string or rope (depending on the size of the basket)

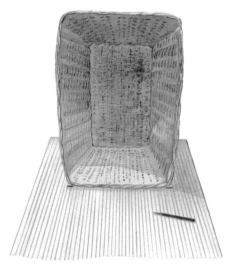

❶ To make a bag, cut four pieces of fabric to fit inside the basket and extend approximately 50cm/19½in beyond. First, lay the ticking reverse-side up on a flat surface. You may like to fold the fabric in half so that you can cut two side pieces and two end pieces at the same time. Next, tip the basket on one end. Position the basket on the fabric with enough room on either side to extend the diagonal lines of the basket by approximately 50cm/19½in. Mark the four outside corners of the basket with a pencil. Remove the basket and join the pencil dots marked on the fabric with a straight edge across the bottom and along each side.

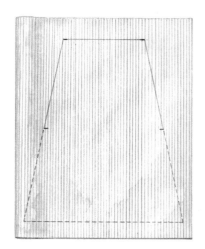

2 Following the diagonals of the sides of the basket, extend the side lines approximately 50cm/19½in beyond the top of the basket, or pencil markers. Join at the top.

3 Now mark a cutting line 1cm/⅜in outside the first (sewing line) shape. Cut out. (You may wish to cut without marking a cutting line. If so, add a 1cm/⅜in seam allowance.)

4 Repeat steps 1–3 to cut out two more pieces for the sides of the basket. Stand the basket on its side and extend the diagonals by about 50cm/19½in, as before.

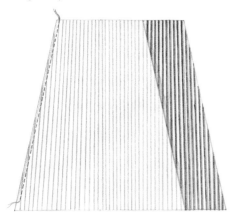

5 Still working on the wrong side, pin, tack and machine-stitch along the sewing lines, end to side piece, until all four pieces are sewn together. Stop 6cm/2⅜in below the top on every seam. This gap will make a turn for the drawstring.

6 Now cut out a piece of fabric for the bottom of the basket. Stand the basket on the reverse side of the fabric. Mark all four corners with a pencil. Remove the basket and join the dots. This is a sewing line. Adding a 1cm/⅜in seam allowance, cut out the fabric.

7 Line up the bottom sides of the bag with the sides of the base fabric, right sides of fabric together. Pin, tack and sew together. Sew to the ends of each sewing line.

8 Pin, tack and machine-stitch the ends of the base fabric to the bottom ends of the bag, again sewing to the ends of the sewing line. The bag is complete.

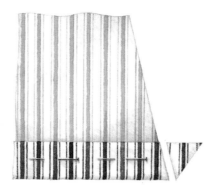

9 To make a channel for the drawstring at the top of the bag, tuck under the cut edge of the fabric for a neat finish and turn back on the inside of the bag approximately 2.5cm/1in. Pin in place. Trim the excess fabric corners in line with the diagonal sides of the bag.

10 Sew the top seam by hand and remove the pins. If machine-stitching, tack the seams and remove the pins before sewing. At each corner, tuck in each cut end of fabric and sew in place, taking care to leave an opening for the string or rope to pass through.

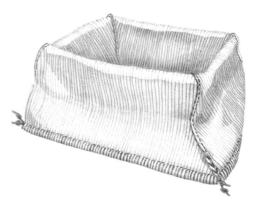

11 Cut two lengths of string or rope for the sides. Make the lengths as long as the sides, plus enough to make a substantial knot at either end. Cut two lengths of string for the ends in the same way. Knot one end of the string, thread the other end through the relevant side or end of the bag, and then knot the remaining end. (If you have difficulty threading the string through the channels, attach the end of the string to a safety pin and push the pin through.) Using four lengths of string allows each panel to be opened and pulled to individually.

tool
store

This carry-all ensures that small garden tools, twine and seed packets are within easy reach for simple gardening chores. It can be tied to a garden bucket or the front of a wheelbarrow between the handles, or even worn around the waist. Made from plastic-coated cotton, it is easy to wipe clean, and touch-and-close seams open out flat so you can expel any lingering soil or stray seed.

you will need:

45 x 65cm/17½ x 25½in plastic-coated cotton or medium-weight pvc

Double-sided sticky tape

Scissors

Approx. 12 self-adhesive touch-and-close dots

Approx. 2m/2yd string

Large safety pin (optional)

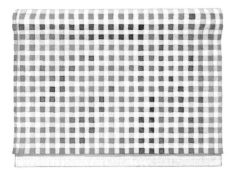

1 Lay out the length of fabric right-side down on a work surface. Fold the fabric down almost in half lengthways, leaving about 2cm/¾in of reverse fabric showing.

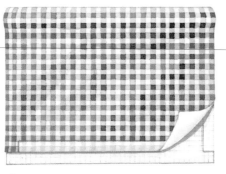

2 Lay double-sided sticky tape along the bottom width of the uppermost face and along each inside edge, stopping approximately 2cm/¾in short of the top fold.

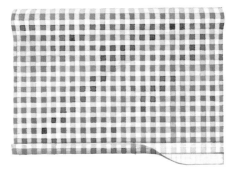

3 Peel off the waxy top tape and seal the fabric on both sides. Fold up the bottom section and press firmly onto the uppermost face to seal the fabric on all three sides.

4 Position garden tools on top of the sealed fabric with the handles extending beyond the top fold. Turn up the bottom half of the fabric to approximately 2cm/¾in short of the fold. Use pins to mark seams between each tool. Mark the line of the bottom fold and the position of the top flap, approximately 2cm/¾in short of the top fold.

5 Remove the tools and open out the fabric. Divide and stick six touch-and-close dots along each vertical seam, including outside edges, taking care to marry positive and negative dots.

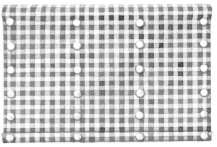

6 Now fold the fabric along the line of pin markers, align the touch-and-close dots, press firmly and remove pins. To tie the tool store to a bucket or wheelbarrow, loop the two lengths of string, approximately 100cm/39⅓in in length, to thread through the top fold of fabric. If the tool store is to be worn around your waist, tie a length of string loosely around your waist to find the correct length, cut another identical length and loop the two lengths together.

7 Thread two ends of the same piece of string through the top fold of the fabric so that the loop sits in the middle of the fold. If this is difficult, attach the two ends of string to a large safety pin and push it through. Tie the tool store to a bucket or wheelbarrow and lightly gather the fabric over the string so that the pockets do not lie completely flat.

shower **curtain**

This is an inventive and practical way to store everything you need for a shower. Shampoo, sponges, brushes and shower gels slot into convenient pockets that range down the inside of a shower curtain. Items can be left in the pockets after you have finished showering. Stack personal toiletries at a handy level for individual members of the family – child-friendly shampoos and gels can be placed within easy reach for children; teenage lotions and potions somewhere in the middle; and adult oils and specialist products at the top. The pockets are angled for easy access, storage and effective drainage, and open stitching means that any water in the pockets will drain down into the shower tray or bath. If you are using fine plastic shower curtains, do not overload them as they may tear with the weight of the items. Alternatively, for extra strength, use a plastic-coated fabric shower curtain.

you will need:

Shower curtain and rings

Dressmaking pins

Chalk (or dressmaker's pencil)

Ruler

Nylon thread or fine fishing line

Needle with a large eye

Scissors

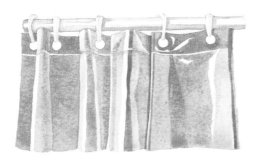

1 Hang up the shower curtain and double up the last two hooks, turning the end inward toward the shower to create the pocket flap.

2 Consider what items you want to store in the pockets and where. As a guide, line up on the floor any bottles and sponges you use every time you have a shower. Position items according to the heights of family members.

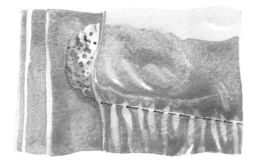

3 Working from the top of the curtain, mark the seam for the first pocket. Push dressmaking pins through the double-thickness of the folded shower curtain. Begin at the turned-in edge and make a gradual diagonal line down toward the outside fold. Insert the uppermost bottle or accessory and leave it in place.

4 Slide the second bottle or accessory into place below the first pocket. Check that there is enough room for easy access. Mark the position of this item with a pin for the second seam, and put the bottle or accessory to one side. Pin a diagonal line to mark the second seam, as before, and put the bottle or accessory back in place.

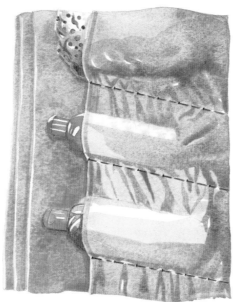

5 Continue down the shower curtain, marking pockets for items. Leave everything in place as you work and be careful not to overload the fabric. Finer plastic shower curtains will hang out of shape and may tear if overloaded.

6 Empty the pockets. If you feel confident sewing the shower curtain in situ without a pencil line as a guide, leave it hanging and ignore the next step. Otherwise, take down the shower curtain and move to a work table.

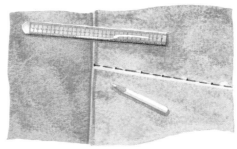

7 As a guide to stitching, stitch sizes and to getting a neat diagonal, use a ruler and chalk marker at this stage. Place the ruler just under the line of pins. Using the chalk marker, make 2cm/¾in dashes along the ruler. This broken line will be a guideline for running stitch. A 2cm/¾in stitch length is ideal to allow easy drainage.

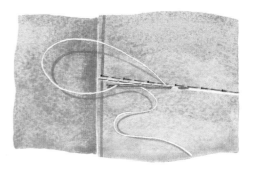

8 Leave the dressmaking pins in place. Now, using nylon thread, begin sewing from the opening of the pocket, securing the end of the nylon thread with a good knot. Stitch along the pencil line and knot again at the fold. Use transparent or white nylon thread for a simple style, or use a colour if you want a decorative contrast.

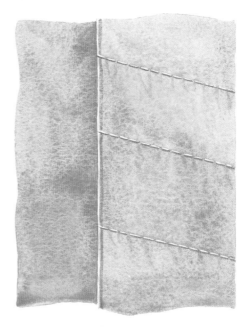

9 Continue down, sewing all of the seams in this way, leaving the pins in place until you have sewn each seam. Once each seam has been sewn, remove the pins.

vegetable
store

This hanging vegetable rack is a practical
way to divide and store fresh vegetables.
Its multi-tiered construction means it is
easy to see which vegetables you have in
store, and it can be dismantled for cleaning.
The holes in the colanders allow air to
circulate around the vegetables and help
maintain their freshness, so this design is
good for storing root vegetables such as
potatoes, onions and turnips, salad foods and
fruit. The colanders used here are medium-
size, which limits the vegetables to an
appropriate weight for the chain and hooks.
If you want to increase the size of colander
and storage capacity, simply use heavier
chains and hooks and secure a firm fitting
to the ceiling or kitchen rack.

you will need:

*As many colanders (metal or plastic) as you want for
your store – each 24cm/9½in diameter*

1 x "S" hook

*Hook to attach vegetable store to ceiling (or butcher's
hook to hang store from kitchen rack)*

*Bolt cutter to cut chain, pliers and pinchers to
open chain*

For every colander:

2 spring hooks or carbine hooks

*Approximately 100cm/39in of chain. (Take exact
measurements when you buy the chain – you may be
able to get it cut to length at the suppliers)*

1 Measure the distance from the ceiling or kitchen rack to where you want the first colander to hang. Cut two lengths of chain to this length and join the pieces at the top with the "S" hook. This hook can loop onto a ceiling hook or butcher's hook suspended on a kitchen rack.

2 Connect the other ends of the two lengths of chain to the handles of the colander with spring hooks or carbine hooks.

3 To hang the second colander, hold it below the first in position, and measure the distance between the two. At this stage you will find it easier to add additional colanders if you hang up the first. If you are not ready to hang the vegetable store in its place in the kitchen, use a butcher's hook to hang it on a washing line or in a doorway.

4 You will now need to cut two more lengths of chain, to the measurements determined in step 3 above. Attach each end of chain to the spring hooks on the first colander.

5 To create the second tier of your vegetable store, connect the ends of the chain to the handles of the second colander with spring hooks.

6 Your vegetable store is now complete. If you require more storage, you can add one or two more colanders with chains and spring hooks.

Alternative: Instead of measuring and cutting chains yourself, you can use ready-made kits for garden hanging baskets. Such kits supply three chains for every basket, whereas this technique requires two chains – so remove one of the chains with pliers and pinchers or a bolt cutter.

roller
store

Anything from magazines and books to lap-top hobbies like knitting or Nintendo can all be stored neatly and conveniently in a personalized roller bin. Wheel the bin alongside your chair when you put your feet up and store it out of the way behind the sofa or under the television table when not in use. Choose a bin that fits in with your interior decoration.

you will need:

Bin

2 cake presentation boards (square or round to fit into the bottom of the bin)

Glue (appropriate to the type of bin)

Drill

2 nuts and bolts with washers

4 castors with screws to fix to the depth of 1 cake presentation board

Screwdriver

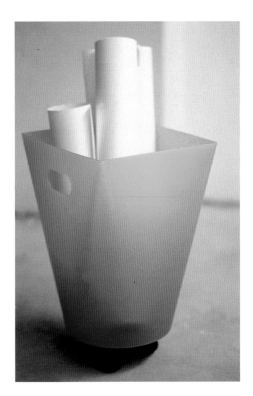

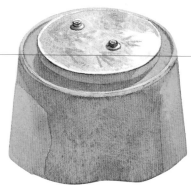

1 Turn the bin upside down and glue a cake presentation board onto the bottom. Follow the glue manufacturers' instructions.

2 Turn the bin so that it is in an upright position again, and fix the second cake presentation board inside in exactly the same position as the first. Stand a weight inside the bin on the board – a teapot, for example – and leave the glue to dry.

3 When the glue is dry, secure the new base by drilling two holes through both of the cake presentation boards and through the bottom of the bin. When drilling, sit the bin half-on and half-off the end of a table – or perhaps a garden step. Drill through the side half-off the table or step first and then rotate the bin and drill a hole in the opposite side.

4 Secure the base by inserting two nuts and bolts through these holes – through both cake presentation boards and the bottom of the bin. Position the nuts on the outside of the bin.

5 When the cake presentation boards are firmly fixed to each other and the bin, fix the castors to the outside cake presentation board only. Position each castor evenly around the outside edge of the cake presentation board and draw around each castor fixing. Working on one castor at time, mark one screw hole and fix, taking care that the screw is the right size to penetrate the outer cake presentation board only. Realign the castor if necessary, mark the remaining screw holes and fix. Repeat for the remaining three castors.

basics

kitchen
planning

There is no set plan for designing a perfect kitchen. Begin by assessing your requirements for equipment and storage (ie. do six people sit down at the kitchen table every day, or two people once a week?), and take into account existing architecture. Choose a practical scheme to maximize space and create a welcoming environment.

Beginning with simple ergonomics, position key activity areas within an imaginary compact triangle – conventionally, kitchen sink, cooking facilities and fridge. Provide ample work surfaces in between or adjacent to each area and incorporate no-fuss storage for equipment, cookware and tableware within easy reach. Store pots and pans next to cooking facilities and knives and chopping boards next to a food preparation surface. Install good lighting throughout, paying special attention to high visibility cooking and work surfaces.

The illustration opposite of a single line kitchen extends along a 3m/3⅓yd wall and contains the essential elements. Use this as a guide to ergonomics and general planning. For anyone with a disability or mobility restriction, consult your local authority, consumer advice office or relevant charity for specialist advice.

1 An industrial-style stainless steel trolley with shelves is a versatile addition to a busy or compact kitchen. Incorporate a permanent space underneath a work surface to store away the trolley when not in use and maintain a clear thoroughfare.

2 The top shelf of a trolley provides a useful "back-up" work surface, or storage space for pans or cookware. Alternatively, fit the trolley with a good-size chopping board or piece of marble for food preparation.

3 Secondary shelves on trolleys can provide permanent storage for pots, pans and cookware. Wheel out next to a cooking area for easy access or line-up alongside a work surface to make a practical L-shape.

4 Leave everyday electrical appliances like kettles and toasters on display on a work surface or convenient solid shelf for easy access. Position them next to an existing or new electrical socket and trim leads, or if possible, rewind onto the appliance to cut down on excessive visible wiring.

5 Inserting a hob in a work surface with a separate single oven below is space-efficient and offers flexibility to mix and match gas and electrical appliances according to personal preference. This arrangement leaves enough space below the oven for a drawer for baking trays, large pans or chopping boards.

6 Store kitchen knives, cutlery and utensils in a slim-line drawer unit, with everyday items in the top drawers for convenience and specialist items below. In standard-size drawers fit dividers or lift-out plastic trays and keep knives and utensils in separate compartments.

7 An open metal or wooden shelf on wall brackets can store cooking oils, everyday food items and spice jars – all within easy reach of a cooking or food preparation surface. It is also convenient for stacks of plates, cups and glasses.

8 Decorative and functional, hanging storage for saucepans and stainless steel utensils provides direct access to everyday equipment for busy cooks, and keeps work surfaces free for food preparation. Suspend a metal rail with secure wall-fixings every 75cm/30in (every 50cm/20in to support cast iron or copper pans) and add an array of butchers' hooks.

9 Leave a section of a hanging rail free for tea towels and oven-proof cloths.

10 Areas next to sinks and hobs are key food preparation surfaces. In a compact kitchen line-up, with sink and hob alongside each other, incorporate a good-size work surface and keep it free from electrical appliances or general clutter. If space is too tight for an adequate work surface, install a hob with a lid to double as a work surface, and fit a wooden board over the sink. Alternatively, fit a retractable board under a work surface or keep a simple folding table or trolley to hand.

11 To match the style of surrounding kitchen units or fittings, fix a fascia or decor panel to appliance doors. All appliances fit underneath a standard 90cm/35½in work surface, apart from mini appliances. If you require a work surface at a different height, fix an independent work surface with wall battens and brackets or stand it on metal or wooden legs. Do not sit an independent work surface on top of units without any fixings, as it will not remain stable. With mini appliances under a standard-height work surface, use the extra space for a drawer or storage basket.

12 Store a flip-top bin out of the way under a sink. It is convenient for vegetable trimmings or peelings and for throwing away waste food before rinsing plates.

13 For an inexpensive recycling system, use a selection of mini plastic bins or buckets for bottles, aluminium cans and paper. Alternatively, use specialist recycling bins with individual compartments for waste products.

14 Store basic cleaning equipment and bucket in an undersink cupboard. Use any extra space above the bucket to fix a simple shelf for storing cloths, brushes and sponges. Or, hang the bucket on a hook on the side of the cupboard.

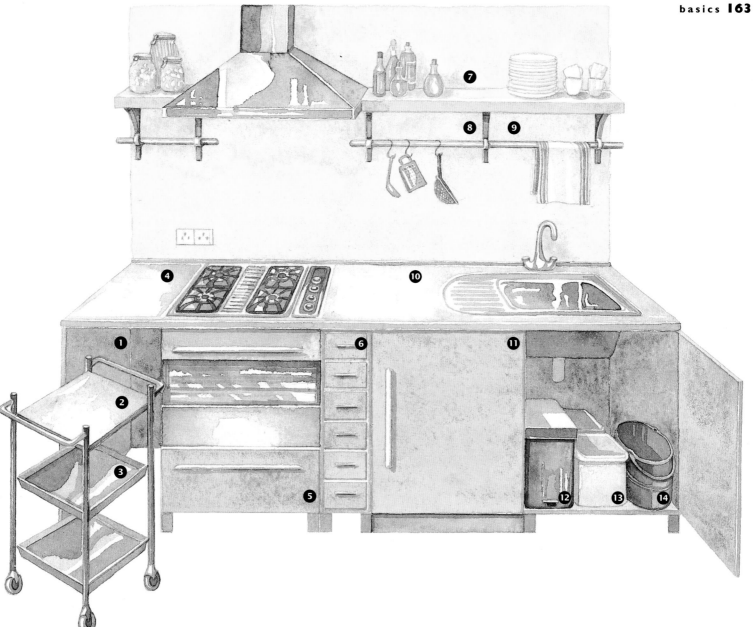

1 Storage space for trolley

2 Trolley with work surface

3 Shelf for bowls and cookware

4 Work surface for small electrical appliances etc

5 Oven with drawer below for baking trays etc

6 Drawer system for cutlery, cooking knives and utensils

7 Open shelf for oils, spice jars and everyday food items

8 Steel or wooden pole with butchers' hooks

9 Storage space for tea towels and oven cloths

10 Work surface for food preparation

11 Fridge with fascia panel in keeping with units

12 Undersink flip-top bin for kitchen waste

13 Individual plastic buckets for recycling bottles and cans

14 Cleaning bucket and equipment

closet
planning

The illustration opposite shows a one-wall flexible storage system for clothing – easily adaptable to fit individual needs. To assess your needs write an inventory of clothing, and anything else you want to store (such as sports equipment). Alternatively, lay out items of clothing and divide them into piles as a guide to how much hanging space and how many shelves to allocate. Incorporate extra space for new acquisitions – add an extra one-quarter to the total storage area to accommodate this.

Organization and flexibility inside a wardrobe is the key to workable clothing storage. Use ready-made units or modular systems with optional infills for a practical arrangement of hanging rails, shelves and drawers. Alternatively, put together an inexpensive system using vertical tracks and adjustable shelves, hanging rails and self-assembly drawer units. Once you have established these basics, fit doors, sliding panels or roller blinds or drapes on a curtain pole.

Use this general guide to measurements when planning space-efficient storage, although you should always check measurements on specific items and, if mixing different sizes of clothing, base measurements on largest jacket and shoe sizes.

1 Store seasonal items such as suitcases, sports rackets or spare blankets on top shelves. Leave this space open for maximum flexibility. As a safety precaution, avoid storing heavy items or boxes out of reach on high shelves.

2 Store shoes in boxes to help maintain their shape and protect from dust and scratches. Use white or unbleached tissue paper to stuff toes, and wrap suede, patent or special finish shoes individually or use plastic or cedar shoe trees. For quick access, store shoes either without boxes on shelves, on slanting shoe racks underneath hanging clothing, or in canvas shoe organizers on the inside of cupboard doors. Loosely knot together the laces of sports shoes and canvas pumps and loop over simple hooks.

3 Fold and pack clean out-of-season clothing in large cardboard boxes with lids, and stand boxes on the floor or base of a cupboard. To prevent possible discoloration or damage, do not stand these boxes next to a heating pipe or radiator. Layer each box, placing heavy items (jackets, coats or woollens) on the bottom and lightweight items (shirts and T-shirts) on top. Use tissue paper to interline and protect delicate or special items or fold carefully inside a plain white cotton or linen pillowcase.

4 Separate individual hats with plain tissue paper and store several in a box to maintain shape and protect from dust, light and moth damage.

5 Store bags and briefcases, including sports sacks and overnight bags, in shelves with upright dividers. Snap or zip shut all bags and stuff leather or satin types with tissue paper to maintain their shape.

6 Fix a hanging rail in a space 60cm/24in wide for coats and dresses – allow 4–8cm/1½–3in of rail for every item and a 150cm/59in drop. This drop will not accommodate floor-length dresses and coats, so either pack these in tissue paper and boxes, loop across two coat hangers or measure individual items and allocate longer hanging space. Alternatively, sub-divide a hanging space with a vertical wooden panel or post and fix rails at different heights. Use brass rails for maximum weight capacity and support every

100cm/39in. To protect items from dust or discoloration, store them in canvas clothing bags with a transparent front or window to identify contents. To prevent possible moth damage for everyday clothing, hang odour-free moth deterrents or cedar balls so that air can circulate around them.

7 Jackets and shirts require 100cm/39in of hanging space. Allow approximately 2–4cm/1½–3in of rail space for each shirt, 4–6cm/1½–2½in for a cotton or linen jacket and 6–8cm/2½–3in for a woollen or tweed jacket. Wire hangers are ideal for cotton shirts. Use satin or cotton padded hangers for linens, silks and woollens or cover wire hangers with tissue paper to avoid marking fabric. Include a carousel hanger for ties and belts or hang them on hooks inside the cupboard door.

8 Allow 100cm/39in of hanging space for trousers, skirts and separates and 4cm/1½in of rail space for every item.

9 Use drawers to store underwear, socks, belts and scarves. For extra organization, insert drawer dividers and store pairs of socks or tights in separate compartments ranging in colours from light to dark. As an alternative to drawers, slot plastic baskets into open shelving or hang a canvas shelf system from a rail.

10 Store rarely used items in spare boxes on top shelves. Line airtight boxes with felt for dress jewellery and beads. Store precious items in individual felt or brushed cotton drawstring bags or mini safes.

11 Lie shawls, throws and fake fur wraps in loose folds on a wide open shelf. Alternatively, use this space for extra pillows, sports equipment or luggage.

12 For easy access and logical storage, divide jumpers and shirts into different colours and stack three or four items in open shelves or boxes. For extra protection from dust or for delicate items use plastic or canvas storage envelopes.

13 Store jeans, T-shirts and casual clothing in open shelves or boxes and fold or roll to avoid creasing.

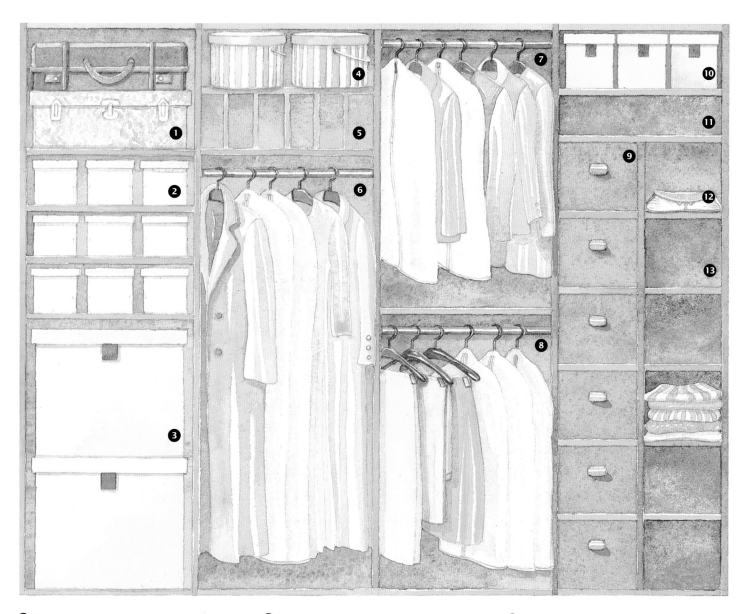

1 Open shelf or space for luggage

2 Open shelving for shoe boxes or shoe bags

3 Storage boxes with lids for out-of-season clothing

4 Hat boxes

5 Bags in individual upright slots

6 Hanging rail for long dresses and coats

7 Hanging rail for jackets and shirts

8 Hanging rail for separates, skirts and trousers

9 Drawers for underwear, T-shirts, belts and scarves

10 Open shelf for extra storage boxes or spare blankets

11 Open shelf for throws, scarves and shawls

12 Open boxes for shirts and jumpers in envelopes

13 Open boxes for jeans, T-shirts and casual clothing

creating
storage

Fixing brackets

As a rough guide to choosing a bracket, find one that will support three-quarters of the width of a specific shelf. Fix brackets every 75cm/29½in along the length, although this measurement will differ depending upon the materials that you use for the shelf and what you plan to store or display. For example, solid wood shelves with a depth of 2cm/¾in require a support bracket every 45cm/17½in. For melamine or chipboard shelving, use a minimum 1.5cm/½in shelf depth or fix a wooden facing to the front of the shelves to prevent bowing.

The key to a secure shelf is a good fixing on the wall with adequate support. If you change the use of the shelf, always review the position of the brackets. For example, if you fix a kitchen shelf to store glasses and, over time, decide to stack dinner plates or saucepans instead, add more brackets to compensate for the increase in load.

Measure the shelf and work out an even spacing for the brackets. If you plan to use part of the shelf for hi-fi equipment, part for CDs and part for ceramics or artefacts, divide the shelf into sections and space brackets evenly within each section – with less space between brackets for the hi-fi section and more space between brackets for the CD section. Make a note of any measurements and check that they all add up to the shelf length before you begin drilling any holes. Always check the construction of a wall prior to putting up shelves – as some walls are not adequately loadbearing.

1 If you know exactly where you want a shelf, you can set about measuring straight away; or position the shelf by measuring from the floor. Alternatively, hold the shelf in place and make a faint pencil mark on the wall directly under the shelf. Put the shelf to one side.

2 To fix the first bracket, line up the top of the bracket with the shelf pencil mark. Make a pencil mark through the uppermost fixing on the wall-mounting part of the bracket. Put the bracket to one side, drill a hole on the pencil mark, insert a wall plug and screw the bracket in place, allowing a little "give" for re-positioning. Sit a spirit level on top of the bracket and make any adjustments before marking the subsequent fixings for the wall mounting.

3 Depending on the design of the bracket, you may be able to tighten the first screw and leave the bracket in place for the other fixings. Alternatively, slide the bracket to one side, drill the holes and tighten all screws when all fixings are in place, after a final check with a spirit level.

4 Fix all remaining brackets. Either lay the spirit level on top of the first bracket and support the other end

with the second bracket, or hold the shelf in place with the spirit level sitting on top and mark the position for the second bracket in this way.

5 Mark and fix one bracket at a time. Once all the brackets have been secured to the wall, sit the shelf in place and, using a pencil, mark the position for the screws through the shelf-mount part of the brackets. If you want to make holes in the shelf for electrical leads, mark the position for these also.

6 Remove the shelf and drill holes on the pencil marks for the shelf fixing, taking care not to drill through the shelf. Drill any other holes for electrical leads. Replace the shelf and fix.

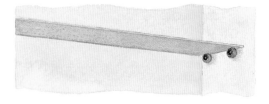

Alternative shelving

A glass shelf with four rubber doorstops instead of brackets in each corner can be an attractive alternative to traditional shelving. Spanning across alcoves (approximately 75cm/29½in wide), with rubber stops as supports on side walls, the shelf is ideal storage for a range of small-scale items including CDs, books or medium-weight artefacts. Use strengthened (or minimum 6mm/¼in-thick) glass, and drill bits and wall plugs that are in keeping with a specific type of wall – for example, masonry or plaster board. Screws should be three times as long as the rubber stop – two-thirds of the length of the screw for internal fixing and one-third to hold the rubber stop in place.

1 Hold the shelf in place and mark a pencil dot on the back of the side wall underneath the shelf – approximately one-fifth of the width of the shelf away from the back edge of the shelf.

2 To fix the first rubber stop, put the shelf down and line up the centre-top of the rubber stop with the pencil dot. Push the pencil through the middle of the rubber stop and mark the wall for the first drill hole. Drill the hole, insert a wall plug and screw the rubber stop in place.

3 To fix the second rubber stop on the same wall, hold the glass shelf in place resting on the first rubber stop and place a spirit level on the glass across its width. Check the level and mark a pencil dot on the wall underneath the shelf one-fifth of the width away from the front outside edge of the shelf.

4 Put the glass to one side and proceed as before. Line up the centre-top of the rubber stop with the pencil dot, push the pencil through the middle of the rubber stop, and mark for drilling and fixing. Fix rubber stops on the opposite wall of the alcove and, after each fixing, hold the shelf in place to check it is level (using a spirit level) before making the next mark.

5 Fix non-slip adhesive pads on the underside of the glass in line with the rubber stops to prevent the shelf from slipping, and slot the shelf in place.

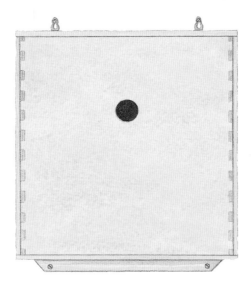

Mirror plates

For use in supporting and positioning traditional wall cupboards and units, mirror plates hook onto screws or nails in a wall. For extra support, fix wooden battens to the wall under the cupboard or unit to take weight off the mirror plates. The batten can be as long as the unit or, for a less obtrusive effect, fix two short battens. Usually mirror plates are unseen; either the top of the cupboard or shelf unit is above eye level or items on the shelf conceal the fixings. If the mirror plates are on view and you want to disguise the brass finish and wall screw, apply an undercoat suitable for metal finishes and paint the fixing the same colour as the wall. Protect the cupboard or shelf unit with masking tape when you paint, or paint the mirror plate before you fix it.

To fix a storage box with pull-out drawer to the wall with mirror plates:

1 Work on the back of the box. Measure a quarter of the length in from either side and make pencil marks. These marks are the points at which to fix the mirror plates.

2 Position one brass mirror plate over a pencil mark so that the top of the mirror plate to be fixed onto the wall sits above the top of the box. Push the pencil through each screw hole on the part of the mirror plate to be fixed to the box and make marks. It may be possible to screw directly into the wood without drilling first. Fix the mirror plate to the box, and repeat for the second mirror plate.

3 Hold the box against the wall and sit a spirit level on top. When the box is level and in position, make pencil marks through the uppermost hole in the mirror plate (the plate slides down the wall fixing to rest at this point). Fix one screw to the wall, leaving enough of the screw head proud to allow the mirror plate to slide behind. (You can tighten each screw onto the mirror plate at the end to make sure it is secure.) Hang the box on one screw, supporting the opposite side. Sit a spirit level on top, and check the marker for the second screw before fixing.

4 If you plan to fix battens to the wall for extra support, hang the box and make pencil marks directly underneath, in line with each mirror plate. Put the box down. Use these marks to position a single batten or two smaller battens. Line up the top of the battens with the marks, and drill through either end of the battens into the wall. Insert wall plugs into the wall before fixing the battens in place with screws. Alternatively, line up the top of the battens with the pencil marks, mark directly underneath again, and put the battens to one side. Drill into the wall directly in the middle of the pencil marks on either end of the battens, and insert plugs. Drill identical holes through the battens, measure to check the position, then fix to the wall with screws.

5 Rehang the box. Drop the box gently onto the battens and tighten the screws on the mirror plates. If you are hanging a shelf in this way with a batten underneath, you can screw down through the back of the shelf into the batten. Be careful to avoid the wall fixings.

safety and storage **advice**

When contemplating your storage options, it is important to bear in mind basic safety points and practical elements. An extensive checklist follows, which includes general advice and safety precautions for each area of your home.

Over and above specific instructions supplied by the manufacturer, always adopt the safety measures specified on page 169 if you plan to undertake a do-it-yourself project, or when moving or assembling furniture.

Kitchens

● Always store cleaning equipment and chemicals out of reach of children. If you choose to store cleaning equipment in an undersink cupboard, always fix a lock or safety catch on the door.

● Knives, scissors and any hazardous utensils or electrical equipment should be stored out of reach of children.

● Keep a fire blanket in an accessible place in the kitchen in the event of a pan or cooking fire.

● Never hang tea towels or cloths from butchers' hooks or hanging rails above hobs or cooking facilities to avoid any risk of fire.

● Do not install hobs or cooking facilities next to blinds or curtains. This can present a fire risk.

● To avoid any risk of fire, do not install wall cupboards or shelves above hobs or cooking facilities.

● Stacks of china should be stored on open shelves in single stacks for convenience and to avoid overloading – for example, keep stacks of dinner plates, soup plates and cereal bowls separate on a shelf. Always dry crockery thoroughly before stacking it.

● When storing precious china, wrap each item individually in fabric sleeves or insert a sheet of corrugated paper or cotton wadding between each plate.

● Silver cutlery is easily tarnished by light, damp and acid in wood, so ideally it should be stored in a cutlery roll. Alternatively, use a length of felt and lay an item of cutlery at one end, roll and cover, insert another item of cutlery and continue this process until all items of cutlery are bound together. Tie the bundle with ribbon or string to keep it intact.

● Do not mix silver and stainless cutlery in the same cutlery tray (and separate them in dishwasher cutlery trays) as contact with stainless steel will damage silver.

● Water and electricity do not mix – to avoid splashing and the risk of damage to an electrical system or worse electrocution, do not position electrical sockets next to a sink or water supply.

● Avoid cupboard doors opening outward into a kitchen and blocking a thoroughfare. Use two doors instead of one, a sliding panel or shutter – or move the cupboard.

● Pay special attention to the position of dishwashers and beware of dishwasher doors obstructing or restricting movement around the kitchen.

● Shelves fixed above eye level should only be used for lightweight, rarely used items; use a set of steps to remove anything. Do not attempt to remove any item you cannot see and never pull on a wall-fixing or shelf for support.

● To stabilize trolleys, especially if you are using a trolley as an extra work surface beside a cooking facility, fix wheel brakes on opposite sides of the base.

● Check ventilation requirements before installing any electrical appliance, especially if you plan to conceal it. If in any doubt, call in a registered professional or contact the manufacturer for expert advice.

● Do not attempt to connect a gas appliance yourself. Contact a registered professional or your local gas board.

● Leave irons standing upright to cool before putting away in a cupboard to avoid any risk of fire.

● Allow adequate space between a work surface and wall unit. If space is at a premium, consider fixing open shelves instead of cupboards to avoid the hazard of cupboard doors opening at head height in a compact environment.

● To avoid steam and heat damage (and a possible fire hazard) do not stand kettles and toasters directly underneath wooden shelving.

Bathrooms

● Always store medicines out of reach of children. Either use a specialist medicine cabinet with a lock or safety catch, or secure a conventional cupboard.

● Keep razors, scissors, tweezers and any chemicals or hazardous lotions out of reach of children – preferably in a wall cupboard under lock and key.

● Store bleach or cleaning equipment out of reach of children under lock and key.

Living areas

● Entertainment equipment requires full support on secure shelving – with adequate allowance for wiring and the connections behind. (Fit narrower shelves above for books and artefacts.)

● Do not overload electricity sockets, and bind together or cover electrical wiring to avoid any risk of entanglement or tripping. Look out for plastic sheathing that groups wires safely or consider specialist hi-fi shelving systems with hollow vertical supports to conceal and guide wiring. Alternatively, drill holes through the backs of units and cupboards, and tape or fix wiring to shelves, supports and along skirting boards.

● Do not stand cupboards directly in front of sockets as this obstructs access and can present a hazard.

● If you use a trolley to store entertainment equipment, always disconnect the electrical supply before moving the trolley from one area to to another. (If you forget, the plug will remain in the socket and your T.V. or video recorder will end up on the floor.)

● Avoid overloading shelves with books, equipment or artefacts and store heavy items on bottom shelves.

● Screw or bolt free-standing units to a wall or insert wedges at the base to make sure that the unit cannot tip forward. (A wall unit is a climbing frame to young children.)

● Store photographs in albums, acid-free plastic envelopes or archive boxes and use photographic mounts, as ordinary papers and glues will damage prints over time. Display valuable photographic prints in frames to protect from dust and keep out of direct sunlight to prevent fading, or use non-reflective glass. Negatives require specialist storage in acid-free files. Keep an index for efficiency.

● To protect glass shelves from scratches, use felt pads or cotton mats (on metal feet of hi-fi equipment, wooden or metal artefacts, sculptures or collections of pebbles, for example).

● If you have young children, avoid the hazard of random stacks of any kind of storage boxes as these can be easily knocked over. Instead, slot them safely into an open shelf system instead.

General

● If valuable items are to be stored in a loft or basement, check for leaks and dampness.

● Keep computer equipment in a cool, dry place and away from direct sunlight.

● Store floppy disks for computers in custom-designed boxes, to prevent them from being damaged.

DIY advice

● Dress well for protection when embarking on any DIY project. Ideally, you should wear overalls. In some cases, you may need to wear protective gloves, goggles or a mask.

● Plan each project carefully and check you have all necessary tools and equipment before you begin.

● Read all instructions for self-assembly furniture and keep screws and fixtures safe and to hand in a bowl or plastic bag. File instructions for future reference. Do not attempt to assemble a large item on your own, and assemble in situ if you can.

● Store tools in a dry cupboard or shed to prevent rust, and keep out of reach of children. Store paint, varnish and any chemicals in well-sealed upright tins.

● When fixing shelves or units, always use relevant screws, wall plugs and drill bits. For solid walls use masonry drill attachments and fixings. For stud or hollow walls, use either wooden fixings for wooden studs or cavity fixings for plaster board in between, depending on load capacity. Check with individual suppliers for specific product information and load capacity.

credits

Products featured in this book are available from the following manufacturers and suppliers. For full contact details, see Directory (pages 141–44).

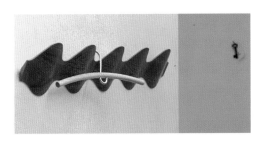

Arc Linea: page 10 (Mediterranea), page 44 (top: Square; left: Gallery table), page 49 (bottom right: furniture), page 54 (bottom left: Biblica system); **Atrium:** page 116 (centre: Atura walnut, black lacquer & aluminium lacquer units); **Century Design:** page 25 (top left: Charles Eames cabinet by Modernica); **Conran Shop:** page 8 (bottom left: Carlo Medera roll-top bureau), page 11 (right: Espiral pivoting drawer stack), page 25 (bottom left: Isokon Penguin Donkey); **C.P.Hart:** page 86 (bottom: bathroom); **Cubestore:** page 138 (Cubekit); **Divertimenti:** page 101 (top right: folding plate rack; bottom right: butcher's block trolley); **English Garden Collection:** page 137 (all pictures); **Futon Company:** page 64 (main picture: Linx storage), page 111 (top: laundry bin); **Goldreif:** page 140 (top: recycling bin); **Habitat:** page 54 (bottom right: Channel trolley); **The Holding Company:** page 68 (top: tie spinner), page 85 (top: three hanging basket hold-all), page 101 (bottom left: wire mesh drawer dividers), page 132 (bottom right: sisal baskets); **Jinan:** page 8 (top right: Stanley cupboard by Dialogica); **Ligne Roset:** page 74-5 (Parallele collection); **Muji:** page 8 (top left: acrylic unit); page 127 (top: storage boxes); **Nick Hill:** page 8 (bottom: airtight food bag), page 11 (top left: journal holder); **Purves & Purves:** page 139 (bottom left: Jasper Morrison bottle crates); **Rick Baker Furniture:** page 90 (top: kitchen design); **Slingsby:** page 96 (bottom right: super erecta shelves), page 111 (bottom right: lightweight Nestaway Truck), page 139 (bottom right: Janitor cart with waistcoat and dolly), page 140 (bottom: four-wheeled container with hinged lid); **The Source:** page 55 (plastic basket); **Viaduct:** page 4-5 (Stacking bookcase by Maarten Van Severen), page 11 (bottom left: Cupboard '92 in aluminium, bakelite and polyester by Maarten Van Severen), page 60 (top left: Alucase by MDF Italia), page 120 (bottom right: Driade mobile unit); **The Water Monopoly:** page 81 (bottom left: Antique bathroom fittings).

pages 42–43
Low table in oak designed by Maarten Van Severen, Viaduct; Franchi shelving system with adjustable shelves in birch ply and Tall Boy drawer unit in MDF with leather handles, Mark Gabbertas; three-tier Klein cupboard, Jinan Furniture Gallery.

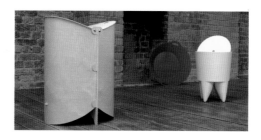

pages 108–9
Double laundry bin in plywood and laundry tub, The Conran Shop; Bubu stool by Philippe Starck, Purves and Purves.

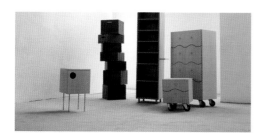

pages 62–63
Peep bedside cabinet, The Conran Shop; Nazanin Kamali bedroom storage unit, Aero; Flow chest of drawers and Ebb bedside cabinet in ash or cherry veneer, part of the Tidal Collection designed by John Whittle, Missing Link.

pages 114–15
Desk in cherry veneer, Purves and Purves; Multiplor desk organiser by Rexite with four revolving compartments, Oggetti.

pages 78–79
Glass cabinet on wheels, Purves and Purves; storage tins, from a selection, Muji; Kartell trolley, The Conran Shop; medicine cabinet, SCP.

pages 122–23
Parallel shelving by Terence Woodgate, SCP; plastic lunch box, Muji; orange CD box, GTC; Ettore Sottsass glass storage jars with red, yellow and black aniline coloured beech wood caps, Oggetti.

pages 88–89
Peg board in stainless steel, Aero; Robo-stacker perforated steel drums with sandblasted toughened glass top, Jam; Parallel shelving in pressed steel designed by Terence Woodgate, SCP; Glass bowl, The Conran Shop.

pages 134–35
Garden sack and trolley and galvanized bucket, from a selection, The Conran Shop.

right A peg board is an ideal way to keep anything from letters and receipts to bills and business cards close at hand. Bulldog clips or pegs are screwed into a chipboard base, and the finished peg board can either be fixed to the wall with screws in each corner, hung like a painting with picture fixings or propped against a wall.

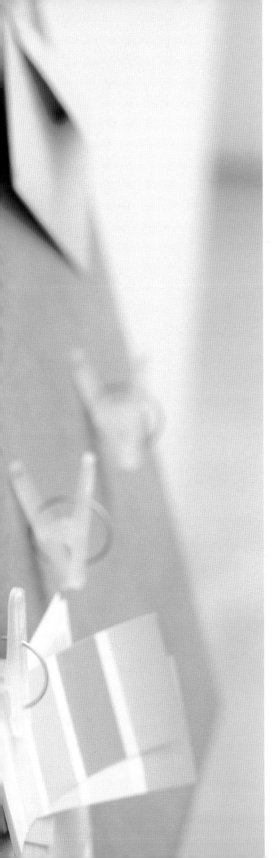

index

acknowledgements

Thank you Simon Upton for your commitment and energy throughout this project, and for capturing a sense of place and light and ease in all your photography.

Thank you everyone at Mitchell Beazley for presenting me with this opportunity and for your collective professionalism.

Thanks to Henry Bourne for kick-starting the New York trip by suggesting I contact Ellen O'Neill and Vicente Wolf. Thanks also to Debra Bourne, Miles Cockfield, Nicholas Coombe, Mats Gustafson, Charles Humphries, Neil Logan, Alfred Munkenbeck and Stefano Tonchi for your vital support.

My biggest thanks to everyone who said yes to photography: Bob Carlos Clarke, P.J. Casey, Tricia Foley, Andrea Gentl and Marty Hyers, Janie Jackson, Markus Kiersztan and Petra Langhammer, Justin Meath Baker and Eliza Cairns, Lysander Meath Baker, Andrew Mortada, Ellen O'Neill, Gunnar Orefelt, Charles Rutherfoord, Annabelle Selldorf, Lisa Smith and Jakob Trollbeck, Ali Tayar, Malcolm Temple, Cesar Vera, Robert Williams, and Vicente Wolf. Thank you for welcoming us.

Thanks also to the following home owners: Ile de Re, François Gilles, Stephen & Gail Huberman, Beverley Jacomini, Jack Larson, Stephen Mack, Issey Miyake, Chris O'Connell, Chuck Rosenach, Sandra Sakarta, Seaside, The Shaker Museum, Tullie Smith House and Stephanie Vatelot.

Thank you to all designers, retailers, press officers, manufacturers and suppliers for loaning products for photography and for providing transparencies of products.

And finally, thank you Lawrence Morton.

Cynthia Inions

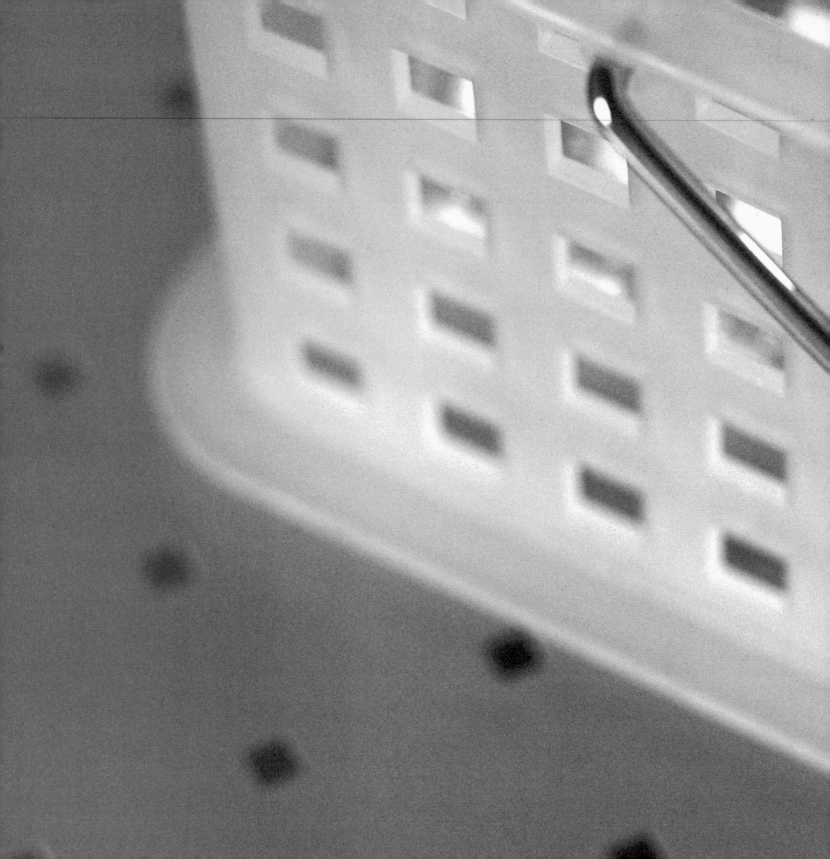